The Genuine Memoirs of Miss Faulkner; Otherwise Mrs. D***L**n; or Countess of H*****x, in Expectancy. Containing, the Amours and Intrigues of Several Persons of High Distinction, and Remarkable Characters

APRIL 1771   No. 693

This BOOK belongs to

H U M P H R Y's

Circulating Library,

CHICHESTER.

UPwards of 900 Volumes,
Pamphlets, &c to let at
Ten Shillings per Year, Three
Shillings per Quarter, or Two-
pence each Volume.

CONDITIONS

No *Subscriber* to have more than
one Book at a time, but at liberty
to change it as often as they like

Readers by the Volume,

for the first Week to pay Two-
pence per Volume, and for each
Week after One Penny

The full Value given for any
Library or Parcel of Books.

THE GENUINE

MEMOIRS

OF

MISS FAULKNER;

OTHERWISE

MRS. D***L**N;

OR,

COUNTESS OF H*****X,

IN EXPECTANCY.

CONTAINING,

THE AMOURS AND INTRIGUES OF

SEVERAL PERSONS OF HIGH DISTINCTION,

AND REMARKABLE CHARACTERS:

WITH SOME

CURIOUS POLITICAL ANECDOTES,

NEVER BEFORE PUBLISHED.

LONDON:

Printed for WILLIAM BINGLEY, at No. 31. in
Newgate-Street. 1770.
[Price 3s. sewed, and 3s. 6d. bound.]

ADVERTISEMENT.

W. BINGLEY thinks it his duty to inform the reader, that the Author of the following Memoirs is mistaken in one material point, namely the marriage of *Miss J———n* with *Mr Fleming*, such an event, he is well assured, never having happened, that gentlewoman being now the Lady of a *Scotch Peer*, and having never been married to any other person. But this is a circumstance, which, it is probable, the Author designedly misrepresented, in order to save the honour of the noble family, with which by her marriage she is now connected; or perhaps, being only a collateral subject, and introduced with the sole

view

ADVERTISEMENT.

view of carrying on the History of *Miſs-Faulkner*, he might think himſelf at liberty to uſe the common licence of a novelliſt, and to ſet it in whatever light might beſt ſuit his purpoſe.

The publiſher returns his moſt grateful thanks to the Authors of the Letters, which he has inſerted by way of *Supplement* at the end of the work, and humbly hopes the faithful manner, in which he has printed them, will intitle him to their future correſpondence.

THE
CONTENTS.

CHAP. I.

CHAP II.

A 3   CHAP.

CONTENTS.

CHAP III.

CHAP. IV.

CHAP. V.

CHAP.

CONTENTS.

CHAP. VI.

CHAP. VII.

CHAP. VIII.

A 4 Faulkner,

CONTENTS.

CHAP. IX

CHAP. X.

CHAP.

CONTENTS.

CHAP. XI.

CHAP. XII.

A 5　　　C H A P.

CONTENTS.

CHAP. XIII.

CHAP. XIV.

I

CONTENTS.

C H A P. XV.

C H A P. XVI.

CONTENTS.

C H A P.

2

CONTENTS.

CHAP. XIX.

CHAP. XX.

CHAP. XXI.

C O N T E N T S.

CONTENTS.

C H A P. XXIV.

C H A P. XXV.

C H A P. XXVI.

C H A P.

CONTENTS.

CHAP. XXVII.

CHAP. XXVIII.

CHAP.

CONTENTS.

CONTENTS.

CHAP. XXXII.

CHAP. XXXIII.

CHAP.

CONTENTS.

CHAP. XXXIV.

CHAP. XXXV.

A SUP-

CONTENTS.

A SUPPLEMENT.

THE

THE

MEMOIRS

OF

MISS FAULKNER,

CHAP. I.

MISS FAULKNER was born in Ireland, about twenty miles from the metropolis, of very honeſt, but very poor parents; whoſe circumſtances prevented their giving her that ſort of education, which the elegance of her perſon deſerved. But it was her good fortune to be the niece of the celebrated *Peter Paragraph* of Dublin; who, having no children of his own, took Mifs Faulkner under his protection, when fhe was about ten years old, and received her from her parents as his adopted child: and Mr. *Paragraph*, being then in very opulent circumftances, and of a really benevolent and generous difpofition, had Mifs Faulkner immediately fent to a boarding fchool, with an appearance fuited to her future education and expectance from her uncle.

Whilft Mifs Faulkner is now laying the ground-work of her future accomplifhments, it may not be difagreeable, or improper, to give fome little account of Mr. *Peter Paragraph*, her uncle, as on him alone all her expecta-

expectations of advancement and support depended after her adoption.

Mr *Paragraph* was born of equally obscure parents with those of his niece, and with some oddities, and some infirmities; of a very low stature, and an uncommonly large head and face, amazingly disproportioned to his body and limbs, and one leg considerably longer than the other, all these circumstances rendered him, what is generally called a very *grotesque figure*; his eyes also were remarkably large, and his voice so much in the *authoritative*, that, with the assistance of an enormous large white wig, with innumerable curls, he has often passed for a *Nabob* in disguise.

The

The obfcurity of Mr. *Paragraph*'s
birth did not, however, deprive him
of an afpiring genius, nor did the
largenefs of his head, fupport the old
proverb. for chance having put him
into the fervice of a printer, who had
fagacity enough to fee into Mr. *Paragraph*'s abilities, he not only inftructed
him in the art of printing, but furnifhed him with fuch further means of
learning as he thought neceffary for
the profecution and management of
his trade and bufinefs ; and as it has
been already obferved, that Mr. *Paragraph* always fhewed an afpiring
mind, he read and ftudied with fo
much affiduity and zeal, that, in a
few years, he exceeded the utmoft expectations of his employer, as well in
the art of printing, as in his knowledge

ledge of the best authors in several languages, and proved himself (in his own style) *a very sensible clever fellow.*

Thus in the high esteem and regard of his patron did Mr. *Paragraph* continue to live for some years, when it pleased the fates to put an end to his master's life and printing at once, and left Mr. *Paragraph* in the peaceable possession of all his business and a considerable part of his fortune.

. Upon this great acquisition Mr. *Paragraph* despised the drudgery of a printing house, and immediately opened one of the most considerable bookfellers shops in Dublin , and the inimitable *Dean Swift* having at that time wrote his *Drapier*, and several

B 3 other

other fpirited papers, Mr. *Paragraph*
procured the printing and publication
of them, and in a few years became a
favourite of the *Dean*'s, at the expence of a laugh, not uncommonly
occafioned by his fingularities, both
of ftyle and drefs, an inftance of
which, we hope, will not be difagreeable to fuch of our readers as love a
joke.

After Mr. *Paragraph* had been
fome time diftinguifhed and greatly
honoured as the Dean's printer and
publifher, by which he had acquired
a confiderable fortune, his gratitude,
as well as his pride, prompted him to
cut a very confpicuous, and confequently a very ridiculous figure on
the Dean's birth-day; and for this
puipofe

purpofe he ordered an elegant fuit of velvet, with a bag wig, fword, and every other apparatus fuited to a man of fafhion, and getting into a chair, fet out for the Dean's houfe, to compliment him on the occafion.—On his arrival the Dean faw him from a window of one of his apartments, and aftonifhed at the folly and foppery of his Printer, was refolved, if poffible, to cure him of a foible he fo much detefted.—On Mr. *Paragraph*'s being introduced to him, the Dean immediately got up from his chair, and with the greateft ceremony received Mr. *Paragraph*, handed him to a chair, and, after the ufual compliments between ftrangers, the Dean afked to whom he was indebted for the honour of the prefent vifit, or if he had any

B 4 commands

commands for him; for he had not the pleafure of knowing him.—Mr. *Paragraph*, not a little abafhed and confufed at this queftion, informed the Dean, that he was Mr. *Paragraph*, *his Reverence's printer*, upon which the Dean, without further ceremony, faid, ' *It was a damn'd lye*; that he knew Mr. *Paragraph*, *his printer*, extremely well; that he was a plain, worthy, good foit of man, and had never made fuch a baboon of himfelf, as the figure before him reprefented; that he was an impoftor, and defired he would inftantly quit his houfe.'—Poor Mr. *Paragraph*, confounded with fuch ridicule, in the utmoft confufion got down ftairs into his chair, and returned home, terribly mortified and perplexed, dreading the confequences of the Dean's fatire and raillery.

He had not been many minutes at home, when a fervant from the Dean informed him, that his mafter defired to fpeak to him immediately on very particular bufinefs. This meffage had well nigh deprived Mr *Paragraph* of his fenfes. He now faw his folly, and dreaded no lefs than a difmiffion from all his employments under the Dean. Great was his fufpenfe, whether he fhould obey the fummons or not; but upon confultation with Mrs. *Paragraph*, who is one of the handfomeft, as well as one of the moft agreeable ladies in the kingdom, and had great weight in all Mr. *Paragraph*'s deliberations; it was refolved, that Mr. *Paragraph* fhould appear perfonally and immediately before the Dean; but not until he had entirely changed

his

his drefs, and re-affumed his week-
day robes.

This point adjufted, Mr *Paragraph* limped off to the Dean's, who
received him with his ufual friend-
fhip and familiarity; and, in feeming
great emotion, told him, that fome
fantaftical puppy had been there a
little before, dreffed in a fuit of velvet, bag wig, fword, &c. and had
affumed his name; "But," fays the
Dean, " I knew *you* too well, *George*,
" to be fo impofed on, I ordered
" the fellow out of my houfe, and
" immediately fent for you, that you
" might be guarded againft this
" impoftor, left he might hurt your
" reputation and credit in the city;
" and I would advife you to adver-
" tife him directly."   3

Mr. *Paragraph* felt the feverity of this irony; but thanked the Dean for his friendfhip; and a fecond time got out of the houfe as faft as he could, well pleafed that it was no worfe. This was, however, a mortifying blow to the pride of Mr. *Paragraph*, who about this time had fome expectations of being dubbed *a knight*, and elected one of the fheriffs of the city, which this unexpected, fatal accident, totally overthrew.

Happy, however, would it have been for the peace, profperity, and grandeur, of the refpectable family of the *Paragraphs*, if this had been the worft confequence, that attended this double difappointment; but, alas,

B 6 who

who can forefee what mifchiefs aic
attendant on even trifling incidents!
We have already mentioned Mis.
Paragraph, as one of the moft beautiful and accomplifhed of her fex;
it naturally follows, that her dear
Mr *Paragraph* (who is one of the
beft judges of the fex) loved her to
admiration (an ample proof of which,
fhall be given in its proper place)
and it unfortunately happened, that
Mrs. *Paragraph* was pregnant at the
time of this difgrace, which fo affected her, that fhe was fuddenly
taken ill, during her hufband's fecond expedition to the Dean's, and
foon after his return home, was delivered of a dead child, a male too!
the hopes, the heir of this worthy
family; and as Mr. *Paragraph* has
never

never since been able to put his beloved in the like condition, the name
and family of the *Paragraphs*, are
now likely to become extinct

As the sympathizing reader is, no
doubt, deeply affected with this tra-
gical story, we shall not dwell longer
on the afflictions of this unhappy
family, than just to observe, that it
was this accident that occasioned the
vacancy, for the adoption of our
heroine, before-mentioned, and as
we now are somewhat better able to
judge of the temper and character of
her uncle and aunt, we shall return to
the adventures of the niece, which
will more agreeably engage our attention in the next chapter.

CHAP II.

MISS Faulkner had been about three years at the boarding-
fchool, where we firft placed her, and had arrived to her *teens*, when fhe gave fuch proofs of her extenfive genius and uncommon underftanding, as aftonifhed thofe who had the care of her education, and exceeded the moft fanguine expectations of her uncle and Mrs. *Paragraph*, who were now become fo equally fond of her, that few days paft in which they did not vifit her, and fhew her every mark of love and affection, which they could have beftowed on their heir, had he lived to enjoy their paternal regards. In fhort, mafters
and

and inftructors in every art and fcience, fit for her tender years, were employed, and fhe excelled the whole fchool in painting, drawing, mufick, dancing, and every other polite accomplifhment; and, in her fifteenth year, Mr. *Paragraph* took her from the boarding-fchool, and brought her home to his own houfe, where fhe continued her amufements, particularly mufick, in which fhe both excelled and delighted.

It may be now thought neceffary, to give fome account of Mifs Faulkner's perfon.—She was fomewhat above the middle fize, but as exactly proportioned, as ever any goddefs was drawn by the pencil of a *Guido* or *Titian*,—her hair, which was as

black

black as ebony, in flowing curls,
covered the fineft neck and fkin in
the univerfe; her eyes alfo were large
and black, with all the *foft languifh-*
ment of the blue, and every turn of
her face, difcovered fome new grace:
add to all thefe natural charms, a
voice that was perfectly tranfporting,
affifted by all the powers of mufick,
and you may, perhaps, form fome
idea of what Mifs Faulkner then appeared to her numerous train of
admirers.   •

A bookfeller's fhop is generally a
place of refort for men of genius, tafte
and gallantry; but the beauty of Mr.
Paragraph's wife and niece, brought
him more vifitors of high rank and
fafhion, than his books, and his
                                    pride

pride always admitted perfons of quality to make frequent vifits in his family; for he was frequently known
to boaft of his extenfive acquaintance
among the nobility, *that he knew lords,*
and lords knew him.

In the number of his noble acquaintance, was Lord K—gs——h, of
gallant and facetious memory; this
young nobleman was as remarkable
for his benevolence, generofity and
hofpitality, as he was for his fpirit of
intrigue, gallantry and debaucheiy;
there never was fuch a compound of
the higheft qualities than can adorn
the human heart, blended with vices
and exceffes, that would difgrace the
moft abandoned profligate: in fhort,
virtue or diftrefs never departed from

his

his door without reward and relief, whilft youth, beauty and innocence, were the daily victims of his moft inoidinate paffions. He was not, by any means, what the ladies pronounce, *a handfome man*: but he was one of the beft bred men in Europe; mafter of the moft infinuating addrefs, and where he once commenced a fiege, was never known to withdraw his forces, until he had full poffeffion of the *citadel*; in the courfe of which he exerted the moft furprizing courage, dexterity, and diligence, when neceffary, and never fpared a profufion of the moft *powerful ammunition.*

No fooner did Mr. *Paragraph* remove Mifs Faulkner to his own houfe, than Lord K———— heard of and

faw

faw her; and as his Lordfhip had a fine tafte for mufick, and play'd on moft fafhionable inftruments in a very mafterly manner, he frequently vifited Mr. *Paragraph*, and fpent feveral hours with his Lady and Mifs Faulkner, in this inchanting amufement; and as Mr. *Paragraph* thought himfelf prodigioufly honoured in the company of his noble gueft, feveral entertainments were prepared, and little parties made at Mr. *Paragraph*'s, in which the whole family were fo delighted with the wit, good humour and elegant behaviour of his Lordfhip, that they were feldom happy but in his company; and, after fome time, his Lordfhip prevailed with Mr. *Paragraph* to attend the ladies to his Lordfhip's houfe, where they were entertained

with

with a fplendor and magnificence, that quite dazzled and confounded them.

This fort of intercourfe was too flattering to the vanity both of Mr. and Mrs. *Paragraph*, to permit them to reflect on its confequences, efpecially as Lord K——— had always behaved in fuch a manner as not to give them the leaft caufe of fufpicion; nor had he, as yet, been in the leaft particular in his behaviour to Mifs Faulkner, more than in the raptures he expreffed at her mufical abilities, and thofe freedoms that are ufual in mufical performances, between perfons of the firft condition.

It is true, that Lord K———. had made fome valuable prefents, fuch

as

as diamond ear-rings, necklaces, &c. both to Mrs. *Paragraph* and Mifs Faulkner, which he prevailed on them to accept, but his Lordfhip had now laid the train, and he was refolved to blow up the garrifon, if he could not take it by furprize or capitulation.

CHAP. III.

LORD K——— had hitherto found it extremely difficult to get a proper opportunity of declaring his paffion for Mifs Faulkner, for in love with her he really and truly was, as his Lordfhip had been with fome dozens before her   and if a few thoufands would have purchafed her fiom either Mr. or Mrs *Paragraph*, he would not have hefitated one moment about entering into the treaty.   But although no man knew the powerful effects of this *magnum bonum*, or the proper methods of applying it, better than his Lordfhip, he had fome reafon to think it would be rejected in the prefent cafe; and if fo, the parties

would

would be more on their guard, and
might poffibly remove his beloved
where he might not be able to find
her : he therefore refolved to proceed
by ftratagem, and to call in frefh
auxiliaries.

In the neighbourhood of Mr. *Para-*
graph lived a lady, whom we fhall call
Mrs. Tabby, the wife of a mercer, who
his Lordfhip knew was not in fo opulent circumftances as Mr. *Paragraph*;
and as this lady frequently vifited in
that family, Lord K——— very
fagacioufly fuppofed, that a few hundreds applied there might be very fer-
viceable to his caufe. To Mrs. Tabby
he therefore applied for her affiftance,
and, after prefenting her with a bank
note, value two hundred pounds, engaged

gaged her to procure him a meeting with Miss Faulkner at her house, unknown to Mr. or Mrs. *Paragraph*; to which Mrs. Tabby readily agreed, and promised his Lordship every affistance in her power. And the better to countenance this defign, Mrs. Tabby that evening met his Lordship at Mr. *Paragraph*'s, when he invited the whole company to fupper and a ball a few nights after. Things being thus concerted, Mrs. Tabby in the interim began to found Miss Faulkner's inclinations in favour of Lord K——— and to her great fatisfaction found, that his Lordship had made fome very tender impreffions on her heart; and in order to touch her to the quick, told her, fhe was informed, that his Lordship was foon to be married to a

young

young lady, whom she mentioned, one of the greatest fortunes in the kingdom of Ireland.

This was a trial, which the un-suspecting Miss Faulkner was utterly unprepared for; and the moment Mrs. Tabby had finished her disagreeable information, she fainted in presence of Mrs. *Paragraph* and Mrs. Tabby, and was some time before she re-covered. And, although the artful tale-bearer well knew the cause of her indisposition, Mrs. *Paragraph* never once suspected it; but having mutually assisted Miss Faulkner, she on her recovery retired to her cham-ber, and, for the first time in her life, felt all the agonies of a love sick heart, on the point of losing the dearest ob-

C   ject

ject of its maiden paſſion ; nor did ſhe
herſelf, until this fatal moment, know
how deeply her affections were engaged to this bewitching, dangerous
lord.

Mrs. *Paragraph* ſpent all the next
day in preparing ſuitable dreſſes for
herſelf and Miſs Faulkner, to appear
in at his Lordſhip's ball, and tho' the
latter would have gladly been excuſed
from appearing there, ſhe knew it was
impracticable; and ſhe prepared accordingly, but with emotions far different from thoſe ſhe uſually went
with to his Lordſhip's entertainments.

It muſt be owned, that young ladies, under thoſe critical circumſtances, are extremely to be pitied.
The

The virgin heart often receives this
fatal impreſſion, when they leaſt
know, or even ſuſpect it, until ſome
accident or ſtratagem forces the diſcovery, and it is then very difficult,
and often impracticable, to prevent or
remove it: but when once this ſecret
is known to the object of their wiſhes,
it in a great meaſure depends upon
his generoſity and honour, whether
they don't fall a ſacrifice, to thoſe *natural impreſſions* and to the impulſe of
that paſſion, to which every human
being is ſubject; unleſs powerfully
protected, and prudently cautioned.
And the inſurmountable difficulty,
which inexperienced young ladies
generally make, of diſcloſing the firſt
impreſſions, of this ſort, on their tender hearts, to ſome friend or con-

fident,

fident, on whom they could with some
safety depend, frequently leads them
to difcover it to low or improper perfons, who proftitute the confidence
repofed in them, and but too often
turn the difcovery to their own private
advantage and bafe purpofes.

While things were thus preparing
at Mrs. *Paragraph's*, Mrs Tabby did
not fail to fly to Lord K————,
and acquaint him with the important
difcovery she had made. Indeed it
was what he before fufpected and
hoped; but he was now in raptures
to hear it confirmed, and by his bounty convinced Mrs. Tabby, that he
would amply reward her future
fervices.

CHAP. IV.

THE night for Lord K————'s
entertainment being at length
arrived, his Lordſhip ſent his own
coach for Mr. and Mrs. *Paragraph*
and their lovely niece, in which Mrs.
Tabby was alſo conveyed. This particular mark of reſpect and diſtinction
from his Lordſhip, almoſt turned the
brain of Mr. and Mrs. *Paragraph*,
and would have been highly pleaſing
to Miſs Faulkner, had ſhe not been
much depreſſed in her ſpirits, and her
little heart flutter'd with ſenſations ſhe
never before felt. 'Tis true ſhe was
dreſſed in the genteeleſt manner, and
in the moſt faſhionable taſte, and the
jewels, that had been preſented to her

C 3   by

by Lord K————, added to her
natural charms, rendered her one of
the compleateſt beauties in the univerſe. She however dreaded, that ſhe
ſhould here meet with her deteſted
rival, whom ſhe now deſperately
hated, tho' ſhe had never-ſeen her ; ſo
that love, jealouſly, deſpair and hatred
alternately ſeized and perplexed her
tender boſom, and almoſt deprived her
of the faculties of ſpeech and reaſon.

In this perplext ſituation ſhe arrived at Lord K————'s houſe ; but
no ſooner had the coach ſtopt, than
his Lordſhip and two or three others of
the nobility, were ready at the door to
receive them   He had previouſly engaged Lord D————, of equal addreſs and gallantry, to attend on Mrs.

Paragraph

Paragraph during the whole evening, and keep up her attention from obferving what fhould pafs between himfelf and Mifs Faulkner; and he had alfo prepaied a perfonage, of the greateft confequence in the kingdom, to engage the attention of Mr. *Paragraph* upon politics, his darling fubject, for the like reafon : fo that he had the coaft quite clear to carry on his operations.

According to the plan that had been concerted, Lord D——— received Mrs. *Paragraph* from the coach, whilft Lord K——— had the inexpreffible pleafure of handing in his adorable Mifs Faulkner; and no fooner had he feized her trembling hand, than he knew the violent emo-

C 4 tions

tions of her palpitating heart and
such is the cruelty of lovers, that, notwithstanding the pain and confusion
which he saw visibly expressed on
her countenance, he rejoiced to know,
that he was the secret cause. He,
however, *whispered soft nonsense in the
fair one's ear*, and in some degree cal-
med her swelling bosom, before they
joined the company.

Lord K——— had previously
acquainted the company, which he
had assembled on this occasion, with
Miss Faulkner's amazing powers in
musick: several of them were nice
judges, as well as Lord K———;
and no sooner were the usual cere-
monies, and tea, &c. over, than
Miss Faulkner was unanimously requested

quefted to play and fing, accompanied
by fome others of the company.
This particular attention to his niece,
for the firft time, drew Mr. *Para-*
graph from his political corner; he
was tranfported with the compliments
every body defervedly paid Mifs
Faulkner; and though fhe feveral
times attempted to play a favourite
fong of Lord K————'s on the
harpfichord, her hands trembled fo
violently, and her whole frame was
fo agitated, that fhe could not proceed: but, in order to oblige the
company, and obey her uncle, who
was particularly preffing on the occafion, fhe requefted Lord K————
would play, and that fhe would endeavour to accompany him with her
voice. This met with univerfal ap-

probation; and she exerted such
powers, accompanied with a tender
plaintiveness in her voice, that every
word of the song, which was immediately applicable to her own situation, sunk into the very soul of
Lord K————; and when the
whole room joined in their warmest
praises, he sat in silent admiration
and delight unutterable. It is impossible for those who have not experienced the powers of musick,
flowing from the lips of a fine
woman, to conceive what Lord
K———— felt upon this occasion,
there is no magic equal to the sounds
of such heavenly harmony; nor is it
possible for human nature to resist
such united charms. Upon this occasion, indeed, Miss Faulkner ex-

pressed

preffed what fhe really felt, with
that modeft confufion and pathetick
fweetnefs, which fent thoufands of
flying Cupids, with their pointed
fhafts, through all Lord K————'s
vital frame : no wonder then, that
his Lordfhip was all tranfport, and
totally abforbed in the moft extatic
blifs.

Several other noble performers
feized the founding inftruments : but
to our heroine or his lordfhip, there
was no mufick, no harmony in their
dull notes. After this concert was
over and fupper ferved up, Mifs
Faulkner began to recover her ufual
vivacity and fpirits. She faw no rival.
Lord K———— had behaved to her
with the greateft tendernefs and re-

C 6   fpect,

fpect, and Mrs. Tabby did not fail to encourage her by every perfwafive fhe could think of, and the company were in raptures with her beauty, wit, and charming behaviour. Mr. *Paragraph* himfelf was delighted with and complimented his moft engaging niece; and when the ball began, which Lord D——— opened with Mrs. *Paragraph*, Lord K——— danced the whole evening with Mifs Faulkner.

During the dance Lord D——— took particular care to draw off Mrs. *Paragraph*'s attention from Lord K——— and Mifs Faulkner; and his Lordfhip took that opportunity of declaring his paffion to his beloved. In fuch a place and fo circumftanced, fhe could not make any reply, which

was

was what he both knew and defired, as he before knew the fituation of her heart, and only wanted to convince her of the ardency of his own paffion; and after faying every thing he thought neceffary for that purpofe, he in the moft earneft manner begged fhe would honour him with a meeting the next evening at Mrs. Tabby's, that he might further convince her, both of his fincerity and regard for her. To this requeft fhe readily confented, and after fpending the evening in the moft agreeable manner, Mr. *Paragraph*, his Lady and niece, returned home, as they came, in his Lordfhip's coach, concluding it one of the moft agreeable and happy days of their lives.

D

C H A P. V.

IT has been already obferved, that
Lord K——————— was compleatly
verfed in all the arts of feduction, intrigue and gallantry, and knew to a
moment when to feize any advantage
he had gained He was, therefore,
determined to lofe no more time in
compleating the prefent defign, than
was abfolutely neceffary; and tho' he
was as abandoned and devoted to his
pleafures as any man living, he always
endeavoured to gain the affections and
regard of thofe very innocents, whom
he afterwards was as fully determined
to feduce and deftroy. And as he
was now convinced he had fully engaged the whole foul of Mifs Faulkner,

ner, he refolved to carry her off, before fhe had time to reflect on the nature or confequence of her engagements in his favour; and for that purpofe had ordered a chariot and fix of his beft horfes, with proper attendants, to wait near Mrs. Tabby's the evening after the ball, that if he could perfuade her to elope with him, it fhould be done inftantly.—Thus prepared he fet out for Mrs. Tabby's, where he found Mifs Faulkner at tea with that *worthy* Lady; and, upon his Lordfhip's entering the room, our heroine was once more feized with her palpitations, and apprehenfions of *fhe knew not what.* However after fome general converfation, Mrs. Tabby retired, and his Lordfhip having declared to Mifs Faulkner, in the moft

passionate

paſſionate terms, that he was the moſt
miſerable man in the world, that he
had not known a moment's happineſs
ſince firſt he beheld her lovely face,
and that there was nothing in his
power to make her happy which he
would not comply with, provided he
might flatter himſelf, that he had the
ſmalleſt degree of her eſteem ; ſhe in-
nocently, but truly, aſſured his Lordſhip, that ſhe entertained the higheſt
reſpect and eſteem for him, but that
ſhe could not hear his addreſſes without the permiſſion of her uncle *Paragraph*; and added, that ſhe was well
aſſured his Lordſhip was then on the
point of being married to a Lady of
birth and fortune, ſuitable to his rank
and quality, and begged he would
not endeavour to diſturb her peace of
mind

mind and humble condition, with which fhe was perfectly contented.

This his Lordfhip juftly conftrued into the warmeft declaration in his favour; and after protefting, in the moft folemn manner, that he never would marry the lady fhe fpoke of, that, if fhe would condefcend to go with him into the country, he would fettle an ample fortune upon her for her life, and that, if he ever did marry, fhe fhould be his choice. He reprefented to her, that the confequence of her refufal would be his marrying the lady fhe mentioned, and that, if fhe remained with her uncle, fhe would in courfe be tied to fome rude, low bred mechanic, who would not only defpife and abufe her lovely

perfon,

perfon, but keep her in a fervile poor
way, where fhe would languifh out .
her life, without tafting thofe luxu-
riant pleafures and elegancies, to
which her wit, beauty and accomplifhments intitled her.   Thus preffed
by love on one fide, by fplendor, im-
portunity and deceit on the other, Mifs
Faulkner was prevailed on, and did
confent to elope with his Lordfhip
into the country ; but had no notion
of fetting off that night, which his
Lordfhip was firmly refolved on, left
fhe fhould more ferioufly reflect on
the bufinefs fhe was going to embark
in, and repent.

Lord K————, however, ftept
out of the room, and giving Mrs.
Tabby fome money, defired fhe
would

would buy fome few neceffaries
which might be wanting to Mifs
Faulkner on the road; at the fame
time he iffued frefh orders to his
fervants, to hold themfelves in readinefs. Thofe mirmidons were fo well
verfed and experienced in thefe ex-
ploits, that they immediately under-
ftood what his Lordfhip was now
about. He always travelled with a
numerous and fplendid equipage,
equally well mounted and armed;
nor had he a fervant in his train,
that would not hazard his life in
fupport or obedience of his Lordfhip's commands, as they perfectly
adored him. For fuch really was
the inchanting addrefs and behaviour
of this noble Lord to all ranks and
degrees of people, that, notwithftanding

ftanding his notorious debauches and
exceffes with regard to women, he
was univerfally refpected and beloved,
wherever he appeared; and thofe,
who the moment before were abufing him, and condemning his profligate life, no fooner beheld him,
than they were ftruck with the general admiration entertained of him
by both fexes, and joined in the
univerfal applaufe that was paid to
his many other noble qualities, and
his acts of princely generofity. On
Lord K————'s return to Mifs
Faulkner, he told her, that he had
fent Mrs. Tabby to buy her a riding
drefs, which he had that day feen,
and was fure would exactly fit her;
and Mrs. Tabby juft then entering
the room with fuch a drefs, his
Lordfhip

Lordſhip requeſted Miſs Faulkner to try it on; and while ſhe was dreſſing, withdrew. Every thing being now ready for his purpoſe, he communicated his deſign to his beloved, and prevailed on her that inſtant to get into his chariot, which was waiting within a few ſteps of Mrs. Tabby's door. Thus our heroine was not permitted even a negative voice; for whilſt his Lordſhip preſſed her to immediate flight, Mrs. Tabby alarmed her with the apprehenſions of a diſcovery, and being forced from the arms of her adorer.

Into the chariot they both got, and the word of command was given, to drive to his Lordſhip's country houſe,

houfe, which is about a hundred
miles from the metropolis   And
whilft they are driving as faft as
fix fine horfes can carry them, we
fhall return to Mr. and Mrs *Paragraph*, from whom we have been
abfent fome time.

C H A P. VI.

MR. and Mrs. *Paragraph*, we have already obferved, were in fuch raptures with Lord K————'s entertainment, and the whole of his behaviour during the laft meeting, that next day they did nothing but vifit all their friends, and acquaint them with the particular honours they had received from his Lordfhip and his noble friends; nor had Mr. *Paragraph* the leaft doubt but he fhould now be honoured with the title of Sir *George*, and that Mrs. *Paragraph* would fhine in the character of Lady *Paragraph*. In fhort, he neither thought nor dreamt of any thing elfe, till he was roufed from thefe

delightful

delightful vifions by the abfence of his niece.

Mrs. *Paragraph* had been out all that afternoon, fpreading her own confequence amongft her mechanical acquaintance, whilft Mr. *Paragraph* was difplaying his folly in a circle of his *common council* friends and companions, and, on his return home, was amazed to find his dear lady in the utmoft perplexity and concern for the abfence of Mifs Faulkner, whom fhe knew her hufband doated on, not only as being his niece and heir apparent, but becaufe that, through her powerful influence and perfonal charms, he expected to acquire thofe dignities, which had long filled his warm imagination, and in the

the purſuit of which Mrs. *Paragraph*
was equally eager.

No wonder, then, that the abſence
of the author of all their preſent and
future bliſs filled them with the moſt
dreadful apprehenſions. Meſſengers
and expreſſes were ſent to every
part of the city, where Miſs
Faulkner had viſited; whilſt Mr.
Paragraph, in perſon, limp'd to Mrs.
Tabby's;—but alas! on enquiry
there, that *worthy* Lady had not
ſeen Miſs ſince the night of the
ball at Lord K————'s. This
almoſt diſtracted Mr. *Paragraph*,
but when all the meſſengers he had
ſent (amongſt whom were a number
of young devils) returned, without
being able to diſcover the leaſt

D   trace

trace of the fair fugitive, Mr. *Para-graph* was no longer able to contain himself, or support that philofophy and fteadinefs of temper, which he had been always remarkable for, and greatly boafted of.

Mrs. *Paragraph* was equally affect-ed, and, for two days and nights, they indulged the moft poignant forrow and affliction: but, on the third morning, they received the fol-lowing letter, which, tho' it did not entirely remove their uneafinefs, acquainted them with the rout Mifs Faulkner had taken, and with whom.

" Dear

" Dear Mr. *Paragraph,*

" YOU are no ftranger to the
"   prefling invitations, which I
" have repeatedly given to your
" worthy Lady, Mifs Faulkner, and
" yourfelf, to favour me with your
" company at Rockingham, wheie
" I fhould have the pleafuie of en-
" tertaining you with thofe rural
" amufements, which your good tafte
" and inimitable fancy would relifh,
" beyond any thing the fmoaky town
" can afford. — Some bufinefs of im-
" poitance, which calls me fud-
" denly to the country, prevented
" my paying the refpects due to
" your Lady and yourfelf, befoie
" my departure ; and, as I could not
" bear travelling alone, I have pre-
" vailed with your adorable niece

" to

" to honour me with her company:
" I have affured her you will excufe
" fo precipitate a departure, when
" you are convinced fhe is under the
" protection of her faithful admirer,
" and

　　" Your moft obedient fervant,

　　　　　　" K——H.

" P S　If Mis *Paragraph* and
" yourfelf will honour us with
" your prefence, I have given
" directions, that a coach with
" a fet, and whatever fervants
" you may pleafe to order, fhall
" attend you to Rockingham."

The receipt of this letter at once
convinced Mr. *Paragraph* and his
　　　　　　　　　　Lady

Lady of the folly of their conduct with respect to their niece, and at the same time blasted all their golden dreams of title, preferment and grandeur. The story immediately became public, and they were both laughed at, and highly cenfured by all their acquaintance, fo that it required fome months to filence the ridicule, before Mr. or Mrs. *Paragraph* could venture again to appear in public.

Reflection convinced Mr. *Paragraph*, that he was much to blame, and that he was in fome degree chargeable with his niece's difgrace; but he was aftonifhed, that Lord K———— fhould thus openly avow the crime he had committed and as fome of our readers may be of the fame opinion,

D 3   we

we fhall, in the next chapter, further
acquaint them with the real character
of that Nobleman, and give them
fome account of his country refidence,
which perhaps may not prove difagreeable.

C H A P. VII.

LORD K———'s father died when his Lordship was about twelve years old He was then at Eton school, where he remained for some time afterwards, till he went to Oxford, and, upon his leaving this last place, made the tour of Europe, and returned when he was about twenty two, in possession of a real estate worth 16000 l. a year, and woods and ready money to the amount of two hundred thousand pounds. In the course of his travels, his Lordship seduced the Lady of a foreign Noble-man, and persuaded her to elope with him to England, and from thence to Ireland, where he supported her with

D 4 the

the utmost magnificence and expence for two or three years, and tho' she was univerfally allowed to be one of the fineft women in Europe, her charms were not fufficient to keep the inconftant heart of Lord K————— folely attached to her. His intrigues and amours became too confpicuous to be concealed from her; and she only defired Lord K————— would permit her to retire to his country feat, where she might enjoy herfelf in thofe rural amufements, which she delighted in; and that she would not attempt the leaft reftraint on his pleafures.

This propofal was readily agreed to by his Lordfhip; for although the fervor of his paffion was entirely abated for this agreeable Lady, he
treated

treated her, in every other respect, with all that decorum, politeness, and every other mark of distinction, that was due to her birth, rank and great accomplishments; and the place she chose for her retreat was Rocking-ham.

It is really a difficult task to attempt a description of this place. Lord K————'s father had expended upwards of sixty thousand pounds in building there one of the finest palaces in Europe, with suitable offices, and other conveniences. It is situated in the middle of a most delightful country, and nature has been more profuse in her bounties to this enchanting spot, than to any other perhaps in the universe Through the

D 5   gardens

gardens runs a large river of the fineft
water, which difcharges itfelf into a
large lake, furrounded by feveral high
hills, covered with pines, oak, and
other woods, for feveral miles : which
affords a profpect diverfified and
beautiful. The lake is feveral miles
broad, and on it his Lordfhip has
built two very elegant fhips of war in
miniature, and by art has raifed an
ifland or peninfula, the exact model
of *Gibraltar*. In the fummer feafon
he frequently entertains his company
on this fine fheet of water, and while
the fhips regularly befiege this little
garrifon, which is defended by a
number of fmall pieces of cannon,
which are very regularly and beauti-
fully played off in it's defence, the
mufick, warlike inftruments, fire-

4   works,

works, &c. form founds and diverfions that are perfectly inchanting.

To this *paradife* Lord K———
conveyed Mifs Faulkner, and on her arrival introduced her to Lady *Valeria*, (which was the name of the foreign Lady already mentioned) who received her with every mark of refpect and efteem, as from the great complaifance, which his Lordfhip fhewed to his fair ftranger, this lady concluded Mifs Faulkner was more than a common acquifition to the *number* of thofe unfortunate beauties, who had vifited this manfion during her refidence here.

You muft not be furprized, gentle reader! at the mention of *numbers*,

D 6   that

that had vifited this manfion of feduction and proftitution; for numbers,
indeed, of innocent pure virgins were
here frequently facrificed, and robbed
of their innocence   For fuch was the
unbridled paffion of this unfortunate
Nobleman, that he conftantly kept in
his pay a whole troop of abandoned,
profligate old women, who travelled,
in different difguifes, through all parts
of the kingdom, and wherever they
faw any prey worthy his Lordfhip's
appetite, they immediately began their
plan of feduction and procuration,
for which purpofe they were conftantly furnifhed with large fums of
money, and never differed about the
price; but if that failed, they reported their endeavours, with a de-
                              fcription.

fcription of the object, when his Lordfhip either perfonally attended, or fent more proper or capable perfons on the enterprize. By thefe means, and the fruits of his own induftry, he never wanted a variety of thefe victims, who were feduced to this houfe, and there dreffed in all the gaudy pomp that can dazzle the weak minds or fuch innocents.

And for the preparing of thefe unfortunates for his embraces, a like number of infernal mations conftantly attended in his houfe, who gave them fuch inftructions and pious documents, that his Lordfhip had no more *trouble than he defired* in the accomplifhment of his unbounded wifhes; nor was it uncommon with him, *in one night*, to

3   debauch

debauch two or three of thefe deluded
wretches, who, from the treatment
they at firft received on their initia-
tion, fine cloaths, delicacies, and the
pleafures with which they were intoxi-
cated, imagined they were landed in
paradife.

Their pleafures were, however, of a
very fhort duration, for his Lordfhip
very feldom vifited any of them a
fecond night, unlefs it were an uncommon beauty indeed, and then the
continuance of a week was an amazing
proof of his conftancy: fuch of them
however, as were afraid or afhamed
to return to their friends or parents,
he fent to a *Seraglio*, which he kept,
for that purpofe, on the borders of
the beautiful lake above mentioned.

To

To others of them he gave confiderable fums of money, fo much at
leaft as generally contented them *for
what they had loft*; and many he had
married to his fervants and tenants,
to whom he generally gave two or
three hundred pounds as a portion,
which, with his former knowledge of
the bride, was an ample fortune.

It may be fuppofed, that his Lordfhip kept this *Seraglio* for his own
gratification, as it was fupported at
a prodigious expence.   There feldom
were lefs than fifty or fixty unfortunate girls contained in it; all of
whom were attended and fupplied,
not only with all the neceffaries, but
all the luxuries of life; a number of
women fervants were kept to wait on
them;

them, and as the greateſt part of them were generally pregnant, phy-ſicians, apothecaries, and midwives, were alſo conſtantly employed, nor was the ſmalleſt neceſſary or conve-nience wanting to any of them   This is mentioned in common juſtice to his Lordſhip, for though he con-ſtantly viſited and inſpected into the management of this *Seraglio*, when in the country, he was ſeldom or never known to treſpaſs on the ſanctity of the place, or any of it's inhabitants, after they had once taken up their reſidence there.

What then, will the reader ſay, could induce him to keep up ſuch an expenſive eſtabliſhment ? It was really and truly for the accommo-dation

dation of his friends. His Lordship fpent the gieateft part of the year
in the country, and, befides a number
of gentlemen that occafionally vifited
at his houfe, he gave a public hunt
once every month, and fometimes
once every week in the feafon. His
general rule was to invite every gentleman that hunted to dine with him,
and confequently to fleep at his houfe;
and as to thofe that he was more in-
timately acquainted with, or chofe to
compliment, he generally afked them
if they chofe *a bedfellow*, which being
ufually anfwered in the affirmative, a
fervant was ordered to attend his gueft
to the *Seraglio*, wheie he might chufe
for himfelf; and when he had made
his option, he returned to his Lordship, and the object of his choice was
immediately

immediately conveyed to his Lordfhip's houfe; and when the gentleman
retired, he found the Lady of his
choice in bed, perhaps dreading,
inftead of impatiently expecting, his
arrival: and according to his Lordfhip's particular efteem, or as a diftinguifhed mark of refpect, every gentleman had a right of precedency in
this vifit to the *Seraglio.*

In further vindication of his Lordfhip's character, it will here be alfo
neceffary to obferve, that none of
thofe ladies durft, upon any account
whatever, accept of the fmalleft
favour, gratuity, or prefent, from
any of his Lordfhip's guefts, on pain
of immediate expulfion, unlefs any
of his friends became enamoured of
his

his bed-fellow, and defired to take her into keeping, which if the lady relifhed, his Lordfhip always confented to, and fhe was directly ftruck out of the books of the convent, and fent to fuch quarters as her lover thought proper.

As to the confequences of thofe nocturnal embraces, his Lordfhip, as has been obferved, employed every needful affiftance; and the number of children, annually produced from this intercourfe, were carefully fent to proper nurfes, and maintained at his Lordfhip's expence, to the great benefit of the community, and the increafe of his Majefty's fubjects.

However

However extravagant this account of Lord K——— may appear, to those who have not before heard of or known his Lord'ſhip, it is literally true, and in this very ſituation was his houſhold at the time Miſs Faulkner arrived there, but as we do not intend to introduce her into the *Seraglio*, or put her on the ſame footing with the wretched medley already mentioned, we ſhall defer what farther remains to be ſaid of her reception at Rockingham, to the next chapter.

C H A P   VIII.

NOtwithſtanding the depravity of Loid K————'s fancy, no man had a higher notion of *delicacy*, in his ſenſe of the word, that is, he placed his higheſt felicity in the certainty of his being a real object of deſire with thoſe he ' moſt ardently wiſhed to enjoy ; nor would he on any conſideration force the inclinations, or uſe the leaſt compulſion in the gratification of his wiſhes. When, therefore, he happened to encounter any young woman above the common claſs, which was his particular delight, his whole ſtudy was to pleaſe, and render himſelf perfectly agreeable, which he thought

abſolutely

absolutely neceffary to render his enjoyment perfectly compleat; nor had
he, in all his various adventures,
ever met with an object, in every refpect, fo fuited to his fancy and
tafte as Mifs Faulkner: and, as he
had now reduced the unfortunate
Lady *Valeria* to the detefted office
of affifting or adminiftering to his
debaucheries, we may readily conclude, that every invention, every
fpecies of luxurious entertainment
and mode of intoxication, was employed to amufe, delight, and fubdue
the prefent object of his flame.
The firft and fecond day, after her
arrival, were fpent in various amufements and fports; and although Mifs
Faulkner could not but forefee and
apprehend the confequences of her
                                    prefent

prefent fituation, yet fhe could not help admiring and approving the delicacy and politenefs of his Lord-fhip's conduct, and fhe was loft between apprehenfion, love, and admiration !—for Lord K———— had in his addrefs, what fome poet finely defcribes —

" ———————— that prevailing gentle art,
" That can with a refiftlefs charm impart
" The loofeft wifhes to the chafteft heart ;
" Rufe fuch a conflict, kindle fuch a fire,
" Between declining virtue and defire,
" 'Till the poor vanquifh'd maid diffolves away,
" In dreams all night, in fighs and tears all day."

Lord K———— was a perfect mafter of this art, and had too often fucceeded in his defigns by the practice of it, when he knew all other

methods

methods muſt fail him. He was convinced this mode. of addreſs was abſolutely neceſſary with women of education, and would prevail, where ruſticity, broad expreſſion and forward obtruſion, would give offence, and render the tranſgreſſor odious and deteſted.

By ſuch inſinuations he had now entirely ſubdued the heart of Miſs Faulkner, ſo that ſhe only breathed, or rather ſighed, languiſhment and deſire. The ſecond night after her arrival, he was determined to grant her no further reſpite; and accordingly gave orders for every preparation for the bridal bed, except the formal ceremony of marriage, which he utterly deteſted. He had requeſted

Lady

Lady *Valeria* to be particularly attentive in her inftructions, and alfo in adminiftering a certain potion of fuch ingredients, as would oblige his charming victim to obey *Love's firft fummons*

Mifs Faulkner was accordingly conveyed to a magnificent chamber, adorned and furnifhed with every thing that could pleafe the moft refined tafte and imagination, but

Nor Hymen, *nor the graces here prefide,*
Nor Juno *to befriend the blooming bride;*
But fiends with funeral brands the procefs led,
And furies waited at the genial bed.

CROYAL.

Thefe lines are fo immediately applicable to the infernal wretches employed on the prefent, and many prior

E occafions,

occasions, that they muft convey a lively picture of thofe fiends who led the devoted Mifs Faulkner to this fcene of her ruin, but fhe had no time, or opportunity for reflection. Lord K——— immediately followed the obnoxious train, and no fooner was fhe undreffed and in bed, than fhe found herfelf in the arms of her dearly beloved Lord.

The *banquet* was too delicious to relate——— So powerful! fo inexhauftible were the charms of Mifs Faulkner, that his Lordfhip's flame was rather encreafed than diminifhed by enjoyment; and the next day they arofe, only to recount thofe extatic raptures which *words cannot exprefs*; but which they, the happy pair, *panted to renew*. In fhort, days, nights, weeks and months
paffed

paffed in this elyfium, and Lord K——— not only thought, but was convinced, *he was the happieft amongft mortals*, and to fill up the meafure of his delight, Mifs Faulkner in due time declared her pregnancy. There was now no bounds to his Lordfhip's happinefs. The moment he was acquainted with this circum-ftance, he ordered a compleat fet of the moft valuable jewels to be made, which he prefented to the idol of his foul, and for upwards of nine or ten months, during which they remained in the country, this inconftant Lord never once tranfgreffed the bounds of fidelity; fo devoted was he to the charms of Mifs Faulkner.

About the end of ten months Mifs Faulkner was delivered of a fine boy,

to the great joy of this noble family,
which however lived but a few days.
Miss Faulkner had suffered inexpreffible torture in her labour, and her
life was in imminent danger for
feveral days, during which Lord
K———— could hardly be kept a
moment out of her room, and was
like a frantic man during her illnefs.
The death of the child was a mortal
blow to the happinefs of both it's
parents. They were both inconfola-
ble, and on the re-eftablifhment of
Mifs Faulkner's health, his Lordfhip
refolved to return to Dublin, which
fhe readily agreed to, as the country
had now loft all it's charms for her,
nor could fhe endure the place where
fhe had loft the tender pledge of her
virgin love.

CHAP. IX.

LORD K——— and Miſs Faulkner returned to Dublin in the winter, and took up their reſidence in his Lordſhip's houſe; and as it was now publicly known, that his Lord-ſhip had this fair prize in keeping, he did not ſcruple to appear with her in all public places; and the ſplendor of her dreſs and equipage, added to the beauties of her perſon, created her numberleſs enemies amongſt her own ſex. Indeed his Lordſhip was profuſe and laviſh in his favours to her; and it was currently reported and believed, that he had not ex-pended leſs than ten thouſand pounds in cloaths and jewels for her perſon in the ſpace of one year.

In

In the meridian of her glory, and at a time, when she and every body imagined that his Lordship was more firmly attached to her than ever, an incident happened, that blasted all her hopes and enjoyments.

About this time it was that Lord K———— became acquainted with the celebrated Miss J————n, daughter to a gentleman of fortune, and much esteemed in the polite world. Miss J———— was deemed one of the greatest beauties of the age, and one of the most accomplished of women. No sooner had his Lordship seen her, than he entertained some hopes of adding her to the number of his conquests—nor was he long in suspense. Miss J———— was grown

to

to the age of two and twenty, and as her father had lived very gaily and expensively, he could not afford his daughter a fortune, suitable to the expectations her rank in life and personal charms flattered her with. She was amorous and sprightly, and with very little solicitation agreed to elope with Lord K———, which she did a few days afterwards, in broad day, and in presence of some hundreds of spectators; and the elopement was performed in the following manner.

Her father's house was immediately adjacent to one of the most public walks, or places of resort, in the metropolis, and it was previously agreed on between Miss J——— and Lord K———, that he should

E 4 order

order his equipage to attend near the
walks that afternoon; that he fhould
appear about five o'clock, and as
foon as he faw her approach, he was
to get into his chariot, and that fhe
fhould follow and immediately drive
off, all which was executed as agreed
on.   And although her father faw her
go into Lord K————'s chariot, he
was not able to prevent their efcape,
his Lordfhip having as ufual ordered
his poftillions to drive as faft as the
horfes could go; and before Mifs
J————'s father could get his horfes
ready to purfue them, they had, by
taking crofs roads and travelling moft
part of the night, eluded his fearch.

They at length arrived at an inn
about thirty miles from town, where,
without

without any ceremony, they ftript
and went to bed, totally indifferent
about what the world might fay of
them, where we fhall leave them, to
indulge a few hours only, and return
to Mifs J————'s father, who never
ftopt riding the whole right, and
having got intelligence of the fugi-
tives in many places on the road, he
at length came to the very houfe
where they were in bed.

This gentleman had been an officer
of diftinction in the army, and tho'
now advanced in years, was a man of
fpirit, and extremely tenacious of the
honour of his family; and tho' attended but with one fervant, he was
determined to oblige Lord K————
to repair the injury he had done his

E 5 daughter,

daughter, by inftantly marrying her:
for this he put a cafe of loaded
piftols in his pockets, and while Lord
K———'s fervants were regaling
themfelves after their fatigue, Mr.
J——— found out the very room
where his Lordfhip lay, and having
fuddenly forced open the door, he
found his Lordfhip and his daughter,
in love's clofeft fierce embrace.

The fight of fo unexpected and
unwelcome a vifitor roufed Lord
K———, when Mr. J. prefented
a piftol to his breaft, and fwore
vehemently, that he would that inftant blow his Lordfhip's brains out,
if he did not immediately rife, and
reftore the honour of his family, by
marrying his daughter.   Lord K———
in

4

in vain expoftulated with the en-
raged Mr. J. for a few minutes,
and what might have happened is
hard to determine, if one of his
Lordfhip's fervants, an old faithful
Swifs, who had lived with him fome
years, had not at that moment rufhed
into the room, and prefented a blun-
derbufs to Mr. J————'s head,
fwearing, in his turn, that he would
blow his brains out, if he did not
permit his Lord to rife and drefs.
This gave his Lordfhip fome time
to think, when he affured Mr J
that if he would go out of the
room until he dreffed, he would wait
on him immediately. The honeft
Swifs obliged Mr. J———— to
comply with this propofal; and having withdrawn into another room,

E 6   Lord

Lord K———— followed him directly, after affuring Mifs J————
that he would not give her up, nor
fuffer any violence to be offered her
by her father, or any other perfon,
at the peril of his life.

As foon as Lord K———— en-
tered the room, where Mr. J————
waited for him, Mr. J———— afked
his Lordfhip, whether he intended to
marry his daughter, to which his
Lordfhip replied, It was the very
firft time he had ever thought about
it, and whatever his intentions might
be on that head, he was determined
that compulfion fhould not influence
them. He did not attempt to juftify
his conduct with refpect to his daughter, but that he was not to be in-
timidated

timidated either by force or menaces.
Upon which, Mr. J——— afked
his Lordfhip, If his piftols were
ready? and his Lordfhip having an-
fwered in the affirmative, Mr. J———
ftood on the other fide of the room,
and fired one of his piftols at Lord
K———————, which having miffed
him, his Lordfhip declined his fire,
but told Mr. J———, that he
hoped he was convinced he was not
to be bullied, or compelled into any
reparation for what had paffed between his daughter and him. He
vowed the greateft regard for her,
and added, that he could not be
provoked to offer any violence to
the parent of one fo dear to him;
and then begged Mr. J——— would
return home, and wait a few days
for the refult of their future progrefs.

Mr. J———n found that Lord K———h, was a man of the moſt undaunted courage, equally cool, enterprizing, and reſolute, and that force would not do with him, and after endeavouring to extort a promiſe of marriage from his Lord-ſhip, which he utterly declined or refuſed to give, and ſeeing all his Lordſhip's ſervants armed, and in readineſs, he found it would be in vain to attempt the recovery of his daughter, and was therefore obliged to depart without her.

On Lord K———h's return to Miſs J———n, he found her in the arms of two or three women ſervants in fits, and abſolutely deprived of her ſenſes; for when ſhe heard the report

report of the piftol, which her father had fired, fhe was certain that either her Lord or her father was killed, nor could fhe be perfuaded of the contrary, until the return of Lord K———h, whofe voice was like a cordial to her fpirits, and helped to revive her. His Lordfhip convinced her that her father was returned home, and that they were both unhurt This account of what had paffed perfectly reftored her; fhe foon recovered her former vivacity, and they fet out in fearch of new adventures; where we fhall leave them, and return to the afflicted and deferted Mifs Faulkner.

CHAP. X.

THE elopement of so conspi-
cuous a character as Miss
J———n with Lord K————h,
and in so public a manner, could
not long remain a secret, nor was
Miss Faulkner one of the last that
heard of it, for early the next
morning, Mr. K—, a brother of
his Lordship's, called upon her, and
in the greatest hurry and confusion
told her the whole story; and added,
that he feared his brother's life was
in the most imminent danger, as Mr.
J———n had the night before pursued his Lordship, with a party of
men all armed; and that, as he
knew the temper and resolution of

both

both parties, he concluded, that
many lives were likely to be loft
on both fides; but could not learn
what rout they had taken. He,
however, fummoned all his own fervants, and feveral of his Lordfhip's,
and immediately fet out in queft of
them.

In this melancholy condition was
our fair fufferer left, and all her hopes
and enjoyments blafted by this fatal
adventure.   She really loved Lord
K————h, and the apprehenfions
fhe was under for his life, for fome
time, engaged all her thoughts and
reflections.   But when fhe confidered,
that he had deferted her for another,
without the leaft fault to be attri-
buted to her, that his affections were
                                    alienated

alienated from her, that she was now left destitute without any means of support, and despised and rejected by Mr. *Paragraph*, on whom she originally depended; resentment, jealousy, and despair, alternately seized her, and she was reduced almost to distraction; nor had she, for three whole days, heard one syllable of what became of Lord K———h, or the detested companion of his flight.

On the fourth day, however, his Lordship's brother returned, and delivered her a letter from her Lord, acquainting her, that business of importance obliged him to leave the kingdom, and that in a few days he intended to be in Paris; that as the

time

time of his return was altogether uncertain, he had given his brother directions in what manner to provide for her, and that she might ever depend on his friendship and sincerest regards.

Every word in this letter was a death wound to the tender heart of Miss Faulkner, nor could she be prevailed on to pay the leaft regard to the future provifion that was intended for her, and propofed at that time by Lord K———h's brother. Her cafe was truly pitiable; and tho' this young gentleman was, by no means, of fo generous or humane a difpofition as his brother, yet he was fenfibly affected with the real anguifh,

grief

grief and defpair, which were con-
fpicuoufly fettled in every feature of
her lovely face.

After many propofals that were
made to her, fhe was firmly refolved
not to remain in that kingdom, where
fhe had fuffered fo much public difgrace; and fhe declared her intention
of fetting out immediately for London: upon which Mr. K————,
furnifhed her with bills to the amount
of 300 l. which was all fhe would
accept of, and only fome part of her
cloaths and jewels; and with this
pittance fhe arrived in London in a
few days, very much dejected in her
fpirits, and in a very poor ftate of
health.

Certain

Certain it is, that if this feparation
had happened in the immediate prefence of Loid K————h, or had he
not been fo critically circumftanced at
that time, that he was really obliged
to leave Ireland, the generofity of his
own heart, and the great regard
which he had for Mifs Faulkner,
would have induced him to make an
ample fettlement on her for her life,
as he had done for others, who were
not, by any means, fo well entitled to
it as fhe was. But, at the preffing
folicitation of his brother, and many
other of his friends, he was prevailed
on to make a tour through France
and Italy, to avoid any further mif-
chief, and until the ftorm raifed by
this laft adventure fhould be a little
blown over. He therefore defired
his

his brother to make only a temporary proviſion for this lady, until his return, not in the leaſt ſuſpecting that her ſpirit or reſentment would ſo ſuddenly operate, or determine her reſolutions until his return.

CHAP. XI.

DURING this tranfaction, Colonel J———n, the brother of
Mifs J———n, was in London;
but Lord K————h had not been
many days at Paris, when he received
a letter from Colonel J———n,
in which the Colonel infifted, that
Lord K————h fhould, imme-
diately upon receipt of that letter,
return to Ireland, where he would
meet him, and expect the ufual
fatisfaction, for the injury done his
fifter. Mifs J———n was prefent
when Lord K————h received
this letter, knew her brother's writing, and immediately fufpected the
contents, which dreadfully alarmed
her;

her; for she dearly loved the Colonel; and it is natural to suppose Lord K——— was equally dear to her. She therefore exerted all her influence with Lord K——— to decline the challenge, as she had every reason to dread it's consequences; but all she could urge was ineffectual. His Lordship represented to her the folly of declining the interview; that he knew the Colonel to be a man of courage and resolution, and that if his Lordship could be *poltroon* enough to refuse the meeting he desired, they must expect he would pursue them to the most distant part of the globe; that a meeting was therefore absolutely necessary, and that he was determined at every event to give him an interview as soon as possible; but

at

at the fame time pledged his faith to
Mifs J———n, that he would, by
every means confiftent with his honour,
avoid doing her brother any bodily
hurt. This point fettled, it was next
determined, that Mifs J———n
fhould remain at *Paris* until his Lordfhip's return, or until fhe heard the
event of this dreadful meeting, as
fhe trembled at the thoughts of feeing
her brother more than at death itfelf.
Now it was, that fhe began ferioufly
to reflect on her folly, and the difgrace fhe had brought upon a family,
before unblemifhed, and valued for
their unfpotted honour; which, together with her feparation from Lord
K———, whom fhe never ex-
pected to fee again, filled her mind
with the moft gloomy apprehenfions.

F　　　Lord

Lord K———— then retired to another room, where he made a will so far as it respected Miss J————n, wherein he charged all his estates with the payment of twenty thousand pounds to Miss J————n, in six months after his decease. With this paper sealed up he returned to Miss J————n, and desired she would take care of it, until she heard further from him; and after giving her unlimited credit at his banker's for her present occasions, he took the most tender and affectionate leave of her, and set out from *Paris* that very afternoon, of which he gave the Colonel notice by express,

Lord K———— arrived in Dublin a few days before Colonel J————n;

and

and when he was informed of the
precipitate flight of Mifs Faulkner,
and the poor provifion which had
been made for her by his brother, he
was touched to the very foul with
compunction and concern for her;
and when he found, that all enquiries after her were ineffectual, and
that fhe had not left any directions
where fhe might be wrote to, or fent
after, and that fhe had not taken one
half of either her cloaths or jewels,
he could not fufficiently admire her
fpirit and generofity, nor could he
help approving her refentment at his
inconftancy and infidelity. He determined, however, to ufe all poffible
endeavours to find out her refidence
in London; and as foon as the important bufinefs, in which he was

then

then engaged, should be settled, he resolved to reward both her generosity and sufferings.

As soon as Colonel J———n arrived in Dublin, he sent notice to Lord K——— that he should expect to meet his Lordship next morning at an appointed place a few miles out of town, and that he would be attended by Lord A———, a particular acquaintance of Lord K———'s, who was punctual to this appointment, attended by Mr. K———, his brother. As soon as these champions were met, Lord K——— desired to know Colonel J———n's commands for him, upon which the Colonel asked his Lordship, if he intended to marry his sister. Lord K———

K——— replied, he verily believed
he never would marry, and that a
thought or a word on that subject
had never paſſed between him and his
ſiſter; that he did not mean to throw
the leaſt reflection on Miſs J———,
but that, in his own vindication, he
thought it then particularly neceſſary
to declare, that he never had, nor
ever would make any promiſe of that
nature to any woman whatſoever;
that if he had made any ſuch promiſe
to Miſs J———, compulſion was not
neceſſary to induce him to perform
it; but as he had never made her any
ſuch promiſe, and as it never had
been mentioned between them, he
did not hold himſelf in honour bound
to any ſuch engagement, and therefore would not give the moſt diſtant

F 3 hope

hope of it. And, after some other conversation on the subject, his Lordship jocularly asked the Colonel, if any one of his Lordship's sisters (and he had then three, very fine young ladies) should take it in her head to elope with him, without previously obtaining his promise of marrying her, whether he thought his Lordship would be mad enough to insist on his fighting him for indulging her; and then declared, upon his honour, that he would not. His Lordship then very judiciously remarked, that there was a wide difference between seducing a young lady under promises of that nature, and without; that he did not think either the laws of the land, or even the laws of honour, required so great a sacrifice as a man's
life,

life, for flying with a charming girl,
with her own free will and confent;
and that if any man was to take one
of his fifters on thefe conditions, he
would not think himfelf in any degree
obliged to call her lover to any account whatfoever for it: but, on the
other hand, if any of them fhould be
feduced under falfe promifes, that he
would, at the peril of his life, oblige
her feducer to perform fuch promifes
as were made her, previous to her
elopement, and that was as much as
the laws of either juftice or honour
required.

Lord K———h had given but
too many proofs of his courage, to
fuppofe he made ufe of thefe arguments from motives of fear: on the

F 4   contrary,

contrary, he then affured Colonel
J——n, that if he was not fatif-
fied with his principles, or if he
thought that he was guilty of any
finifter or unfair dealing with Mifs
J——n, he was ready to give him
whatever fatisfaction he defired; but
that his regard for the Colonel's
perfonal fafety as well as his own,
(as the fate of bullets was very uncertain) obliged him to give his
opinion, and ftate the cafe in the
manner before-mentioned, and he requefted the Colonel would duly con-
fider it, before they engaged in fo
ferious a bufinefs as they were prepared for.

Colonel J——n was as remarkable
for the excellence of his underftanding

ing and his good fenfe, as he was for
his generofity and courage, and was
ftruck with the force of his Lordfhip's arguments, as well as his open,
candid behaviour; and Lord A——
being alfo ftrongly of Lord K——'s
opinion; the Colonel declared, he did
not think himfelf juftified either in
attempting Lord K————h's life,
or rifquing his own, from what had
happened; but with great compla-
cency and good humour told Lord
K————h, that his father was in-
confolable for the lofs of his daughter, whom he loved to diftraction,
and that he would efteem it as a
favour, if his Lordfhip would reftore her to her difconfolate parents;
but that, for his own part, he would
never fpeak to her, or take any

notice

notice of her. This requeſt Lord K——h thought himſelf obliged to comply with; and thus the combatants parted, giving ſignal proofs of their good ſenſe, as well as of the moſt undaunted courage.

CHAP. XII.

LORD K———h had no sooner finished this important business, than he set out for London, in his return to Paris, determined, if possible, to recover Miss Faulkner, and to restore Miss J———n to her parents, agreeable to the promise he had made the Colonel. With this intention, on his arrival in London, emissaries of various kinds were employed and dispatched through all parts of the town, and several days were spent in fruitless enquiries for our heroine.—She had taken lodgings in the neighbourhood of Grosvenor-Square, the most retired and private part of the town; and being.

an entire ftranger, without one fingle
acquaintance, fhe lived in the moft
frugal manner with a widow lady,
to whofe houfe fhe had been recommended; and feldom ftirred out of
doors but in her company, fometimes
to the play, and at other times to
take a walk in Hyde-Park; and in
this obfcurity fhe had paffed feveral
months, fo that it was almoft impoffible to find out her retreat.——
Lord K————h had fpent a whole
week in London, without receiving
the leaft account of her; he continued feveral perfons in employ for
the fame purpofe, during his abfence,
and fet out for Paris.

We muft not, however, too haftily
conclude, that Lord K————'s immediate

2

mediate return to Paris, proceeded
from the violence of his paffion for
Mifs J———n, or that it was in pre-
ference to the pleafure the difcovery
of Mifs Faulkner would have given
him. It was quite the reverfe. Ambition prompted his Lordfhip more
than love, in his adventure with the
former. He never entertained for
her any of that real tendernefs and
regard, which he felt for Mifs Faulkner, and now that fhe appeared loft
to him, all his former paffion for
this lovely fugitive revived with ad-
ditional ardour, and the apprehenfions he was under left any fatal accident had happened to her, filled his
mind with a concern and anxiety
which he never before felt, and he
was refolved to recover her at any
expence

expence or trouble, on his return to London.

These were his principal inducements for immediately setting out for Paris before he had found her; and the promise he had made Colonel J———n to restore his sister, was another motive for his speedy return to that Lady. She was equally rejoiced at his safety, and the attention which he paid her, in so suddenly removing her fears and apprehensions; but after a few days, when he acquainted her with the promise he had made to her brother, she was confounded, and touched with the severest remorse.

Lord

Lord K————— however affured
her, that the Colonel had given him
his word of honour, that fhe fhould
meet with the kindeft reception from
her parents, and that not a fyllable of
what had paffed would ever be mentioned to her, provided fhe returned
to them immediately; and to convince her that thefe were the fentiments of her father, he advifed her to
write a penitential letter to him, and
requeft an anfwer directed to London,
where they fhould receive it on their
return to Ireland, as they would leave
Paris in a few days.

Mifs J————n was none of thofe
inflexible ladies, that languifh out the
remainder of their lives, and dye of
broken hearts for the lofs of their
lovers.

lovers. When ſhe found there was no alternative, and that Lord K——— was determined to part with her, ſhe conſoled herſelf, wrote as he deſired to her father, and after a few days ſpent in viewing all the curioſities at Paris, ſet out for London, as chearful and happy as the nature of her ſituation would permit.

On their arrival in London, Lord K——— reſolved to take ſeparate apartments for Miſs J———n, as well to keep up ſome appearance in her favour, as to prevent the further reſentment of Miſs Faulkner, if he ſhould be ſo happy as to find her. Elegant lodgings were accordingly taken for Miſs J——— in Pall Mall, where a handſome equipage was

ordered

ordered to attend her, with two footmen in her own livery, and as Lord
K——— had purchafed her a great
many very rich and elegant dreffes at
Paris, fhe cut a very confpicuous
figure. This, his Lordfhip knew,
was her darling paffion, and he was
determined to indulge it to any
excefs, in order to divert her from
more penfive reflections. She was
now in as high fpirits as ever: She
had received the moft preffing letter
from her father to return home, and
that every thing fhould be buried in
utter oblivion; but fhe could not
think of leaving London, till fhe had
feen all the public diverfions, and
indulged her natural vanity in the
difplay of her charming perfon, drefs
and equipage.

The

The firſt night ſhe appeared at the play, ſhe drew the attention of numbers of both ſexes. She was really an elegant figure, and the richneſs of her cloaths and jewels, together with the novelty of her face, attracted moſt of the bloods and bucks from all parts of the houſe, amongſt whom was a young gentleman from Ireland, who had ſeen her ſome years before in Dublin, and knew her brother and family; but, having been out of that kingdom for ſome years, had not heard any thing of her adventure with Lord K———, who was then alſo in the houſe, but purpoſely avoided going into the ſame box with Miſs J——— for the reaſons already mentioned. Mr. Fleming, for that was the

gentleman's

gentleman's name, who was now particularly ftruck with Mifs J———'s figure and appearance, feeing her alone and unattended, refolved immediately to make himfelf known to her: but as this accidental meeting is of fome confequence to Mifs J———, and cannot be related in this chapter, we fhall defer it to the next, that the reader and author may have a little refpite, which one of them, at leaft, is this moment in need of.

C H A P. XIII.

IN the foregoing chapter it was obferved, that Mr. Fleming was very much ftruck with the beauty and elegance of Mifs J———, and that he refolved to approach her fair fhrine. He did fo, and was immediately recognized by her.   Mr. Fleming was a young gentleman of very genteel family and connections, and had frequently vifited at her father's, when a ftudent in the college of Dublin.   He had juft entered into poffeffion of his paternal eftate of the value of 1500 l. a year, was but a few weeks returned to England from his travels, and was, what may be called, an agreeable young fellow, and perfectly well dreffed.

Mr. Fleming was particularly pleafed with the affable and polite reception he met with from Mifs J———, nor was her vanity lefs gratified by the affiduity and pio-found refpect of her vifitor, fo that they became not only very intimate, but greatly delighted with each other's company; and as foon as the entertainment was over, Mr. Fleming politely requefted Mifs J———n would permit him to attend her home, which was readily granted.

When they had quitted the box, Mifs J——— requefted Mr. Fleming would call her fervants who were in waiting, when he was very agreeably furprized with the appearance of two footmen in very elegant liveries, and

an

an equipage finifhed in the very firft tafte, in which Mr. Fleming was conveyed to Mifs J———'s lodgings.

It is here to be obferved, that Lord K——— took very early notice of the profound refpect which Mr. Fleming had fhewn to Mifs J——— at the play houfe, and enquired of fome Irifh gentlemen that were with him, who, and what Mr. Fleming was, which being truly acquainted with, he was extremely pleafed, as it would have given him the higheft pleafure to promote this lady's happinefs or preferment, and that too at any expence, provided he was once difengaged from her. He had promifed to fup with her that very night, and had ordered a very

elegant

elegant repaſt from Almack's, but
leſt his appearance might give Mr.
Fleming the leaſt cauſe of ſuſpicion,
or interrupt what he ardently wiſhed
to promote, he went into the Shake-
ſpeare, and wrote a card to Miſs
J———, excuſing himſelf from ſup-
ping with her, at the ſame time hinting
that he knew the gentleman that attended her home, and deſiring that ſhe
would make the beſt uſe of her time,
until he ſhould wait on her the next
morning, and give her further in-
ſtructions what part to act.

Miſs J———n was extremely
well pleaſed with Mr. Fleming's
behaviour and converſation, and on
the receipt of Lord K———h's
card, doubled her aſſiduity to charm
him.

him. Supper was immediately ordered; which was extremely elegant, supplied with the firft wines, and followed by a rich deffert Mr. Fleming was quite tranfported with the affability and fprightlinefs of Mifs J————; and having ftayed with her till after one in the morning, took the moft refpectful leave of her, having firft obtained permiffion to attend her to the opera the next evening.

After the departure of Mr. Fleming, Mifs J————n entered into a more ftrict examination of herfelf, her fituation and circumftances, than fhe had ever before had either reflection or opportunity to do, and, upon full debate and deliberation, fhe found,

found, that Mr. Fleming was not totally difagreeable to her, that if fhe returned to her father, her adventure with Lord K———h was already known, and would become more public, that fhe would not only be pointed at, and infulted by many of her own fex, whom fhe had formerly looked **down** upon, for their gravity and deformity; and that, in all human probability, fhe never fhould be able to get a hufband in Ireland All thofe weighty caufes and confiderations her thereunto moving; fhe was refolved inftantly to fubdue and vanquifh-Mr. Fleming, and bring him into the holy bands of matrimony;—and with this pious determination fhe went to fleep.

G   The

The next morning Lord K——h waited on her to breakfaft; and being informed how matters went on the preceding night, that Mr. Fleming was to attend her to the opera, and finally of her refolution to noofe him; his Lordfhip was tranfpoited with her fpirit and ftratagem; and to convince her of the great regard and efteem he entertained for her, called for the fealed paper, which he had delivered to her at Paris, opened it in her prefence, and read to her the contents.

Mifs J——n, who had been hitherto an utter ftranger to the purport of this paper, which had been fo long in her cuftody, was aftonifhed at the generofity of this noble

Lord,

4

Lord, and expreffed her gratitude for this uncommon inftance of his affection for her. His Lordfhip then declared to her, it was his folemn determination never to marry, but that as he had been acceffary to a misfortune, which in the nature of things, and according to the notions of mankind, muft affect her in her future profpects, he thought himfelf bound to repair any injury fhe had fuftained through his means, in the beft manner in his power; and therefore, affured her, that if fhe could prevail on Mr. Fleming to marry her, he would inftantly raife 10,000 l. and prefent it to her as a portion, fuitable to her quality and merit.

Mifs

Miſs J————n could not be in-
ſenſible of the greatneſs of his Lordſhip's generoſity and goodneſs in this
propoſal, nor was ſhe wanting in
proper acknowledgements. It was
then agreed, that his Lordſhip ſhould
viſit her but ſeldom, and in as private a manner as poſſible, that if
Mr. Fleming, ſhould make any declaration in her favour, ſhe was to
inform him, that the deſign of her
preſent viſit to London, was to receive a legacy of 10,000 l. that had
been left to her by a relation, who
died in the Eaſt-Indies, which
ſhe expected every hour to be paid
her, and that as ſoon as ſhe had
ſettled that buſineſs, ſhe intended to
return to Ireland directly, but that
her return there would afford her

very

very little happinefs, as her father
infifted fhe fhould marry a perfon
every way beneath, and difagreeable
to her, though he was fuperior in
point of fortune, and that fhe expected her brother every day in
London to expedite her return.

This deep concerted fcheme being
thus plann'd, Lord K——— and
Mifs J——— parted equally pleafed,
and with mutual promifes of confidence, advice, and every other
affiftance for compleating their project.

Mr. Fleming the next night,
according to his appointment, attended Mifs J——— to the opera.
She was now refolved to play off all

G 3   her

her artillery upon this unsuspecting
young gentleman, and her designs
succeeded even beyond her expectations, for he became so violently
enamoured of this artful adventurer,
that, on the sixth day after their
acquaintance, he made a formal
declaration of his passion for her,
which she received with the utmost
seeming surprize and confusion; and,
agreeable to the plan that had been
concerted, introduced her legacy, her
father's cruelty, and her brother's
appearance to enforce his commands.

These were stimulatives that Mr.
Fleming did not want, for he was
really and *bona fide* in love with
Miss J——, and would probably
have

have married her without once mentioning her fortune, as he knew her
family, and doubted not but her
father would give her a very genteel portion, if such a thing had
taken place. But when he learned
that she was in danger of being
sacrificed to the embraces of a man
obnoxious to her, and that she had
10,000 l. totally independent, he
thought it was madness to risk
the chance of permitting her to
return, until Hymen had made them
inseparably one. In short, he became
so importunate, and Miss J———
became so pleased with his importu-
nity, and *so fearful of being noosed
to the monster of her hatred,* that in
a few days after she was prevailed
with to let Mr. Fleming obtain a

licence

licence for their marriage, the day
of which was fixed, and every thing
ready for the union of this happy
pair. Lord K———— was no
stranger to all these preparations;
and, agreeable to the promise he had
made his *quondam* fair, he procured
the 10,000 l. which he deposited
in a banker's hands in her name;
and delivered to her the banker's
receipt for it. In the mean time
Mr. Fleming very generously had
made a settlement of 500 l. a year
on Miss J————, payable out of
his estates, in case she should sur-
vive him, which he produced to
her, attended by his lawyer, and
executed in her presence, when she
as generously delivered to him her
banker's receipt for 10,000 l.; and
the

the next day they were married in St. James's Church, immediately set out for Ireland, and arrived there perfectly happy in each other, where we shall now leave them to their future destiny, and return to Miss Faulkner, whom it is time to remember.

G 5

C H A P. XIV.

IT would be doing Lord K——
the higheſt injuſtice to ſuppoſe,
that the buſineſs of the foregoing
chapter, however anxious he was
to ſee it compleated, diverted his
attention from making the neceſſary enquiries after Miſs Faulkner,
for he was really as aſſiduous in his
reſearches for her as ever, but to
as little purpoſe; and tho' he uſed
every means for diſcovering her, he
never could obtain the leaſt intelligence concerning her, which gave
him the greateſt uneaſineſs.

Miſs Faulkner was not, however,
ſo great a ſtranger to his Lordſhip's
reſidence,

residence, as she was to the true sentiments of his heart; for a few days after his arrival in London she saw one of his servants pass by the house she lodged in, which put her into such a tremor and surprize, that she was almost ready to faint. The Lady of the house observed it, and kindly enquired into the cause: but though Miss Faulkner answered her evasively, she was resolved to know whether his Lordship was in town or not, and for that purpose would have pursued the servant immediately, and watch where he went to, but was so affected at his sudden appearance, apprehending he might be in quest of her, that she had not power to stir, till he was quite out of her sight. Convinced

however

however that, if his Lordſhip was in town, ſhe ſhould ſee him in ſome of the public places of reſort, ſhe that very night went to both play houſes and to the opera, but could not obſerve him. She therefore went the next night to Drury Lane, and there beheld her dear Lord in one of the ſide boxes. She was now ſeated in the gallery, and altho' ſhe was ſo anxious to get ſight of Lord K————, ſhe by no means intended to ſpeak to him, or that he ſhould ſee her. She therefore ſet a proper perſon to watch him from the play houſe home, and by that means ſoon found, that Miſs J———— was in London, where ſhe reſided, and the ſplendid manner in which ſhe was kept, all which confirmed her in

the

2

the opinion, that his Lordſhip was attached to her in the ſtrongeſt manner, and that ſhe held him by the firmeſt bonds of affection.

However mortifying this account was to Miſs Faulkner, ſhe had too much ſpirit, either to interrupt their enjoyment, or to upbraid Lord K————h with his infidelity, and was reſolved to bear it with forti- tude and reſignation. But as ſhe had never ſeen Miſs J————n, ſhe was now determined to indulge her curioſity, and, unfortunately for her, went to a houſe directly oppoſite to that lady's lodgings, the very morning ſhe was to be married to Mr. Fleming; where ſhe waited her appearance with all that anxiety, agitation,

agitation, and dread, which it is possible for a woman, in her situation, to entertain at the sight of her rival.

Miss Faulkner had not been placed in the window opposite, above half an hour, when Miss J———n appeared in all her charms and splendor, and dressed in the most costly and brilliant manner, as a bride. This was too much for Miss Faulkner to bear. She was ready to expire at the sight of this fatal beauty; and as her whole dress, as well as that of her servants, indicated her approaching nuptials, she doubted not, but Miss J———n was on that very day to be made the happy Lady K———h. But as we are
generally

generally very defirous to afcertain what, when proved, will give us the moft poignant grief, fhe begged a fervant belonging to the houfe fhe was in, to ftep over and afk one of her fervants, if the lady was not going to be married; and being an-fwered in the affirmative, fhe could not fupport the agonies of her foul any longer, but fainted into the arms of her informer, and relapfed fo continually from one fit into another, that a phyfician was at length called, who pronounced her extremely ill; and ordering a chair, fhe was brought home to her lodg-ings, in a fituation better conceived than defcribed.

On

On her return home she was instantly put into bed, where she remained upwards of three weeks in a
violent fever, and most of the time
delirious, so that there were very
little hopes of her recovery, and
although the gentlewoman, in whose
house she was, had the greatest regard for her, and they had been extremely intimate, Miss Faulkner had
never hinted to her the least part
of her history, nor acquainted her
with her circumstances, and Miss
Faulkner having always dressed very
plain, though genteelly, and having lived with the greatest frugality,
her hostess concluded that her finances
were much lower than they really
were, and began to be under great
apprehensions, lest she should die in
her

her houfe, and that fhe fhould have
the phyfician, apothecary, and the
more dreadful train of undertakers
to pay, befides lofing the money
due to her for board and lodging.
She therefore impatiently waited an
opportunity · of finding Mifs Faulkner fufficiently in her fenfes to be
fpoke to on fuch a fubject, which
fhe at length obtained, and with
great delicacy and difcretion afked
her if fhe had got any money in
her drawers, as fhe was quite exhaufted by the great expence of her
long illnefs.   This reminded our fuf-
fering heroine of what fhe had before entirely forgot or neglected.
She therefore immediately gave her
keys to Mrs. Prefton, for that was
the

the good woman's name, and defired fhe would take whatever fhe wanted out of her drawers.

Mrs. Prefton had always behaved to Mifs Faulkner with the greateft refpect, and entertained a great efteem for her; but when fhe went to her drawers, in which fhe found very near 300 l. befides fome jewels of value, and very rich cloaths, fhe was quite confounded, and began to fuf-pect that Mifs Faulkner was a perfon of diftinction, who had met with fome misfortunes, which induced her to live in that obfcurity; and was confirmed in this opinion from fome expreffions of that young lady's during her illnefs, mentioning her dear Lord, and

and other corroborative circumſtances; ſo that when the doctor next viſited his patient, ſhe deſired him to double his aſſiduity, for that ſhe was a per-ſon of more conſequence than he imagined; and having put five guineas into his hand, he was more confirmed in the belief of what the good woman urged, than he could have been by the Archbiſhop of Canterbury, without the like *proof* of his ſincerity and veracity.

Whether this diſcovery contributed to the recovery of Miſs Faulkner or not, we ſhall not determine; but certain it is, that Mrs. Preſton, as well as the doctor, afterwards at-tended with double diligence; and

in

in lefs than a week, fhe was pronounced to be *out of danger*, though
by no means perfectly recovered.

Is it not time to know what is
become of Lord K————h?

C H A P. XV.

AT the beginning of the foregoing chapter, we parted from
Lord K———— in the greateſt
concern at the many fruitleſs enquiries
he had made after his fair fugitive;
but had he known the ſituation, to
which her anxiety and unextinguiſhed
love for him had reduced her, what
would not his generous, ſympathizing
heart have ſuffered? It was her
greateſt misfortune, that he could
not diſcover the place of her retreat;
for had he then met with her, certain
it is, he would have given her the
moſt ſignal proofs of his love and
eſteem, and tho' he ſhould not have
been able to prevail with her to

return

return with him to Ireland, and
renew their intimacies, he would
have made such an ample provifion
for her, as would have put her
beyond the reach of thofe viciffitudes
in life, which it would feem the fates
had decreed fhe fhould pafs thro',
before fhe fhould be rewarded for
her truth, honour and virtue.

A whole month after the departure
of Mr. Fleming and his Lady,
Lord K——— continued in London, in queft of Mifs Faulkner;
but finding all his enquiries ineffectual, he concluded fhe had not
left Ireland, and in that belief, he
then fet out for that kingdom in
hopes of getting fome intelligence
of her there.

On

On his arrival in Dublin, he fent privately to Mr. *Paragraph*'s to know whether he could give any intelligence of Mifs Faulkner; but that gentleman, with great concern declared, he had never feen or heard from her, fince her elopement with Lord K————; foon after which his Lordfhip retired to his country feat, and was feized with an apoplectic fit, which ended his life and his intrigues in a few minutes.

CHAP. XVI.

THE firſt account that Miſs Faulkner received of Lord K————h's death, was from the public papers, which gave her the greateſt concern; for, notwithſtanding his Lordſhip's infidelity, and utter neglect of her, as ſhe imagined, ſhe ſtill loved him to exceſs, and this ſo ſudden and unexpected an account of his death, filled her with equal grief and ſurprize: and as ſhe had not yet recovered her health, ſince her late indiſpoſition, ſhe relapſed, not into ſo dangerous or violent a diſtemper as the former, but into a ſettled melancholy and dejection of ſpirits, which reduced her almoſt to

a

a ſkeleton, although ſhe was extremely well attended by Mrs. Preſton, who uſed every means in her power to recover her, and treated her with great friendſhip and tenderneſs.

In this deſponding ſituation was Miſs Faulkner, when ſhe went, one fine day, into Kenſington gardens, attended by Mrs. Preſton, for the benefit of the air, and a little exerciſe; and in the walks met Lady Valeria. They were equally ſurprized and rejoiced at this unexpected meeting, and entered into the moſt familiar and intereſting converſation; in the courſe of which, Lady Valeria acquainted Miſs Faulkner with the whole progreſs of Miſs J———n's adventure

H   with

with Lord K————, and her marriage with Mr Fleming, which greatly affected her. But when she was informed of the real sentiments of that noble Lord for herself, the uncommon pains he took to find her out both in London and Dublin, and the unhappiness he expressed at his disappointment, all her former love and esteem for him revived, and gave her such exquisite pain, that she could no longer support it, but fell as it were lifeless into the arms of Lady Valeria and Mrs. Prefton, who, with much difficulty, got her to the coach, which was waiting for them, and in which Lady Valeria accompanied them home, where she grew somewhat better, but was still overwhelmed with grief.

After

After some little refreshment,
Lady Valeria used every means in
her power to comfort Miss Faulkner,
and convince her of the folly of her
present dejection, that there were
many who suffered much greater misfortunes and losses than she laboured
under, of which she herself was an
unhappy instance: and as they had
always found the greatest satisfaction
in each other's conversation, Miss
Faulkner requested Lady Valeria to
favour her with her history, which
she had never heard, and she doubted
not was extremely interesting; to
which that agreeable Lady readily
consented, as she knew it would
entertain and divert her dejected
friend, and at the same time convince
her, that she was equally an object

of compaſſion, and more than an
equal ſufferer, thro' her own folly,
and fatal love for Lord K————.

" MY father," ſaid this Lady,
"   was one of the firſt rank
" of the nobility of Venice, and I
" being his only child, and heir to
" a prodigious eſtate, you may
" ſuppoſe no expence was ſpared on
" my education ; and before I arrived
" at my fourteenth year, many perſons
" of the moſt conſiderable rank and
" fortune paid their addreſſes to me,
" and made propoſals to my father,
" for the honour of his alliance. I
" was, without vanity, one of the
" greateſt beauties in that gay city,
" and as much eſteemed for my wit,
" lively converſation, and good
                        " nature,

" nature, as for thofe acquired ac-
" complifhments, mufick, painting,
" drawing, &c. which, together with
" the immenfe poffeffions that were
" to defcend to me, the high rank
" my father held in the ftate, and
" the antiquity of our family, made
" all the Venetian nobility vie with
" each other in the magnificence of
" thofe diverfions and entertain-
" ments, which were daily prepared
" for me, and for which that coun-
" try is more remarkable than any
" other in Europe. But in the
" whole croud of my admirers,
" there was none that ever made
" the leaft impreffion on my heart:
" all were equally indifferent to me.
" My father was, however, ex-
" tremely defirous of having me

married,

" married, and by himfelf and my
" mother had feveral times requefted
" I would acquaint them, who it
" was, in the number of my fuitors,
" that appeared moft agreeable to
" me, or I fhould like beft for a huf-
" band, as they declared they would
" not in the leaft influence my
" choice, provided it fhould be any
" of the nobility of unblemifhed
" honour; but I affured them, with
" great truth, that they were all
" equally indifferent to me, and
" that I fhould be folely governed
" by their advice.

" My dear parents loved me to
" dotage, and this condefcenfion,
" as they deemed it, fo affected
" them, that they repeatedly affured
" me

" me their fole happinefs depended
" on feeing me the wife of fome
" noble Lord, whofe quality and
" accomplifhments would reward my
" virtue and filial obedience; but
" that they were advanced in years,
" and could not be eafy until my
" happinefs was compleated. My
" father, therefore, informed me,
" that he had the greateft opinion
" of the honour and dignity of
" Count Valeria, a Nobleman of
" the firft Venetian family, and
" although his fortune was not by
" any means equal to the poffeffions
" that would devolve to me, he was
" affured his gratitude, for the
" double advantage conferred upon
" him, would infure my felicity,
" and his attention to pleafe me
" in every thing I defired.

H 4

" Count Valeria had been for
" some time in the number of my
" admirers; and tho' he was then
" near forty years old, he was per-
" fectly agreeable in his perfon, had
" the moft engaging converfation,
" and was highly commended and
" refpected for his probity and
" benevolence in the many important
" ftations, which he had filled in the
" ftate and in the fenate; and as I
" had not the leaft pre-engagement
" or particular regard for any other
" perfon, and was extremely de-
" firous to obey and oblige my
" deareft parents, I readily confented
" to receive his addreffes, as the
" perfon intended for my hufband.
" The joy, which this condefcenfion
" gave my father, is not to be
                " defcribed,

" defcribed, and Count Valeria re-
" ceived it with the utmoft transport
" and delight. Very little ceremony
" was afterwards neceffary; and,
" fatally for me, my youth and
" inexperience prevented my feeing
" or confidering the confequence
" of giving my hand and perfon to
" a man, who had not the leaft
" fhare of my affections, but was
" efteemed merely as the friend of
" my father, and refpected entirely
" from the public report of his
" many great qualities and diftin-
" guifhed abilities. But fo entirely
" ignorant was I of thofe tender
" impreffions, to which I have fince
" fallen a facrifice, and fo wholly
" devoted to the will of my parents,
" that, without the leaft reluctance,

H 5   " and

" and with the moſt perfect indif-
" ference, in leſs than a month, I
" ſurrendered myſelf to the arms
" of the Count.

" The immenſe wealth, which
" Count Valeria received with me,
" and was afterwards to receive,
" enabled him to gratify his am-
" bition and elegant taſte, in the
" magnificent and expenſive equi-
" page, which he purchaſed upon
" this occaſion. His country ſeat,
" which is one of the fineſt and
" moſt antient palaces in Europe,
" was ſtript of all it'ſ old furniture,
" and fitted up with new of the moſt
" ſuperb kinds; and his houſe in
" Venice, which is alſo perfectly
" noble, received the ſame addi-
" tions;

" tions; nor was he lefs profufe
" in the number of the moft va-
" luable and elegant jewels which
" he prefented me with; and tho'
" I had always been ufed to the
" higheft entertainments and moft
" coftly dreffes, his noble fancy and
" generofity exceeded all that I
" had ever feen. In fhort, he en-
" gaged all my gratitude and re-
" fpect, tho' he had never engaged
" my love for him. But of this
" diftinction I was as ignorant as
" himfelf, for I really thought I
" loved him as well as it was
" poffible for me to do, and more
" than any other except my parents;
" and he was perfectly convinced,
" that my efteem for him proceeded
" from the pureft paffion of love.

H 6   " We

" We had been married above a
" year, which I spent in this happy
" indifference and tranquillity, when
" my evil genius brought Lord
" K———— to Venice, in the
" courfe of his travels, and as the
" Count was remarkably fond of the
" Englifh, and frequently entertained
" them at his houfe, the arrival of
" Lord K———— was no fooner
" announced to him, than he imme-
" diately waited on him, and a few
" days after engaged his Lordfhip
" to an entertainment with fome
" others of the Englifh nobility.
" He accordingly came, and the
" whole company were charmed with
" his wit, fprightlinefs, and good
" humour; and as I had learned
" to fpeak Englifh from my infancy,

" and

" and Lord K———— could not
" fpeak Italian perfectly, he, with
" the greateft politenefs, requefted I
" would be his interpreter, which,
" with his turn of good humour,
" tinctured with a little gallantry
" towards fome ladies that were
" prefent, highly diverted the com-
" pany, and pleafed me—to my
" fhame I own it—but too much.
" In fhort, the whole day and
" evening was fpent in the moft
" agreeable manner; and after the
" Count had, with great civility,
" preffed the honour of Lord
" K————'s company, as often
" as he could difengage himfelf—
" his Lordfhip withdrew.

" After

" After the company had de-
" parted, and the Count retired with
" me to bed, he could not dif-
" courfe of any thing, or any body,
" but this agreeable Lord. He
" faid, he had met with many
" Englifh gentlemen diftinguifhed
" for their politenefs and education,
" but had never feen any fo per-
" fectly accomplifhed as Lord
" K————, and for fome time
" we joined in our encomiums upon
" his many agreeable qualities. For
" my own part, I had his image
" before me all the remainder of
" the night, and the next morning
" the Count having fent a polite
" card to enquire after his Lord-
" fhip's health, on my going down
                                    " ftairs

" ftairs I was very agreeably fur-
" prized to fee his Lordſhip in con-
" verſation with the Count, all joy
" and life.

CHAP. XVII.

" IT was juſt at this time that
" the Carnival at Venice be-
" gan, and Lord K——— ac-
" quainted the Count, that he was
" that evening engaged to a maſ-
" querade ball at Count P———'s,
" and on my huſband's telling his
" Lordſhip that we were both en-
" gaged to the ſame place, Lord
" K——— begged I would let
" him know my dreſs, and continue
" to him the honour of my interpre-
" tation; which, together with let-
" ting him into the cuſtoms and
" intrigues of Venice, would lay
" him under the higheſt obligations,
" to which both the Count and
" myſelf readily conſented."

" At the ufual time we went to
" Count P———'s, and I was fur-
" prized that Lord K——————— was
" not to be feen in the rooms, but
" in lefs than half an hour he made
" his appearance in the character of
" an Englifh failor, which he filled
" with fo much wit, and fupported
" with fo much fpirit and vivacity
" during the whole evening, that
" the company, and particularly the
" ladies, were in raptures with him;
" and as he was frequently feen in
" familiar converfation with Count
" Valeria and myfelf, it was imme-
" diately known that he was a per-
" fon of quality, and my acting the
" part of his interpreter, upon many
" occafions, drew upon us the at-
" tention of all the fprightlieft
perfons

" perfons of both fexes wherever we
" moved.

" There is not in the univerfe a
" place, where intrigue, gallantry
" and pleafures of every fort, are
" carried on or indulged to a higher
" degree than at Venice during thofe
" carnivals, which are annually
" kept; nor are the *belles paffions*
" there managed or conducted with
" that delicacy and difcretion, which
" they are carried on with in this
" country. It was, therefore, pub-
" licly rumoured and believed, that
" I had adopted Lord K———
" for my *Cicifbeo*, which is the
" cuftom in that country for almoft
" every married woman of any
" fashion."———*Cicifbeo!* fays Mifs
Faulkner,

Faulkner; I don't know what that
means, and but that I would not interrupt your agreeable ftory, fhould
be extremely glad to have it explained to me. Lady Valeria fmiled
at her ignorance, and proceeded
thus.

" The order of *Cicifbei* was firft
" inftituted at Genoa, but the
" fafhion is now fpread all over
" Italy. Thefe are gentlemen, who
" devote themfelves to the fervice
" of fome particular married lady,
" and are obliged to wait on her
" to all public places, fuch as plays,
" opera's, mafquerades, &c. and
" attend her as lacquies, devoting
" their whole time and fortune to
" her fervice. When at home, they
                                    are

" are conftantly with thofe ladies
" in their moft retired apartments,
" where even their hufbands are
" refufed admittance; and as they
" have thofe frequent opportunities,
" you may eafily guefs how the
" ladies reward thefe attendants;
" but their hufbands are not to have
" the impudence to fuppofe this in-
" timacy proceeds from any other
" caufe than pure platonick friend-
" fhip."

" 'Tis true, every hufband endea-
" vours to give his wife a *Cicifbeo*
" of his own chufing, (which was
" my cafe) but when the Lady hap-
" pens not to be of the fame tafte,
" which is frequently the cafe, fhe
" never fails having one of her own
" fancy;

" fancy, and any hufband that
" would be unreafonable enough to
" refufe or be offended at it, would
" be deemed the moft ignorant
" ftupid wretch in the univerfe, and
" excluded all polite affemblies.   In
" fhort, I believe the firft intention
" of this inftitution of *Cicifbei* was
" rather that they fhould be a kind
" of fpies or watch upon the ladies
" than lovers . but the cafe is now
" otherwife, and if a Lady is known
" to difmifs one of thefe gentlemen,
" and engage in any new gallantry
" with another, the difbanded heroe
" is obliged, by the cuftom and
" nature of his office, to refent the
" injury, and either cut the throat
" of his rival, or have a fword run
" through his own body ; fo that
                                    " thefe

" thefe *Cicifbei* are now the guaidians
" of their miftreffes honour, and
" obliged to refent all their quaiiels
" and affionts, inftead of their huf-
" bands, which you will allow is
" fome confideration for the favours
" they fuffer their ladies to beftow
" upon thefe champions.

CHAP. XVIII.

"COUNT Valeria had ap-
" pointed one of this order
" of *Cicifbei* to attend me, but so far
" was he from having any private
" intercourse or intimacy with me,
" that I detested him, as I was al-
" most constantly pestered with his
" company, as well at home as
" abroad, and although he had
" never made any attempt on my
" honour, nor ever declared any
" particular passion for me, except
" the usual compliments of gal-
" lantry, which the nature of the
" office authorizes; yet I could per-
" ceive, that he entertained some
" thoughts of that nature, and my
                              " youth,

" youth, no doubt, inflamed and
" flattered his hopes of fuccefs.
" This *Cicifbeo* of mine was a young
" Nobleman of diftinction, and the
" only fon of one of the greateft
" fenators, of the family of *Can-*
" *taria*, not ungenteel in his per-
" fon, but haughty, paffionate, and
" revengeful ; and as he attended
" me at the ball, feemed very un-
" eafy at the intimacy which ap-
" peared between me and Lord
" K———h; and as we fre-
" quently difcourfed in Englifh,
" which Cantaria did not under-
" ftand, his jealoufy conftrued every
" word that paffed, into a declara-
" tion of love, or a private affigna-
" tion. And as I obferved before,
" that his conftant attendance on me
" was

" was extremely difagreeable, I will
" own to you, that I took a parti-
" cular pleafure in mortifying him,
" and for that reafon indulged feve-
" ral little airs and compliments
" to Lord K————h, which I
" fhould not otherwife have done,
" for although, I believe, that danger-
" ous companion had even then made
" fome impreffion on my heart, I
" did not know it, or fufpect my
" falling virtue; and I confidered
" the pleafure, which I took in his
" company and converfation, as pro-
" ceeding only from the high fallies
" of wit and humour, which per-
" petually flowed from him, and
" with which every other perfon
" feemed as much delighted as
" myfelf.

I   " Having

" Having stayed at the masque-
" rade till five in the morning, I
" was, as usual, attended home by
" Cantaria, who hinted, in presence
" of my husband, that he believed
" I had fallen in love with the
" agreeable English Lord, from the
" particular compliments which I
" paid him, and although he men-
" tioned it in a jocular manner,
" and it was received as such by
" Count Vaicita, I could easily dif-
" cern that he spoke it with a ma-
" licious design, and to punish me
" for the uneasiness I had given
" him at the ball, but my husband's
" presence prevented my replying
" to him, as I should have done
" at that juncture.

" The

" The next night I was at the
" opera; and as soon as Lord
" K————h came into the houfe,
" I could obferve him looking
" through the boxes very attentive-
" ly to difcover me. I made him
" a fignal with my fan to come
" into my box. This put Cantaria,
" who was with me, out of all
" patience; and as foon as Lord
" K————h approached, he with-
" drew, to my great fatisfaction.
" His difpleafure at Lord K————h's
" entrance was fo confpicuous, that
" his Lordfhip took notice of it,
" and afked me the reafon, which I
" incautioufly, and, I am forry to
" fay, very imprudently told him.
" I do not know whether Lord
" K————h then put that con-

" ftruction

" ftruction upon this information,
" which men of gallantry and in-
" trigue generally do on intimations
" of the like nature; or whether he
" came defignedly, or prepared, to
" make a formal declaration of his
" paffion for me, but we had not
" been half an hour together in the
" box, when he convinced me, that
" I had engaged my heart but too
" much in his favour, and that he
" was a moft enterprizing and art-
" ful feducer. He reprefented to
" me the injury done to my honour
" by placing Cantaria as a watch on
" my actions; the abfurdity of being
" under the direction of a perfon of
" fo mean a character; the inequality
" of my hufband's years, and the
" cuftom of the ladies of quality;

" with

" with many other fophiftical argu-
" ments, which entirely fubdued my
" weak underſtanding; and preffed
" me to a private interview with ſo
" much ardour, that unfortunately
" for me, I confented to it; and the
" next day fent one of my women
" to him, to concert meaſures for
" our meeting. This artful woman
" I found perfectly experienced and
" accomplifhed in the bufinefs of in-
" trigue, and as Lord K———h
" was as bountiful, as he was inge-
" nious and enterprizing, my con-
" fidant returned to me in raptures,
" and with the plan fettled foi our
" affignation that very night, in
" lodgings which they had taken
" for the purpofe, in a retiied gen-
" teel

I 3

" teel part of the city. We ac-
" cordingly met at this fatal place,
" and from that moment commenced
" my misfortunes.

CHAP. XIX.

" AFTER this meeting my huf-
" band became odious to me,
" fo that I could fcarcely behave
" to him with common civility; and
" I pofitively infifted, that Cantaria
" fhould withdraw his attendance
" on me. The Count, who only
" lived to pleafe and oblige me, tho'
" he was aftonifhed at this fudden
" change in my temper and difpo-
" fition, readily confented to remove
" this troublefome attendant, and he
" was forbid the houfe, which gave
" me the greateft pleafure; and as
" my hufband had not the leaft
" fufpicion of my honour, I had
" every opportunity I could wifh of
I 4   " meeting

" meeting Lord K——— at the
" place of affignation, which we
" never failed to do every night.

   " We continued our fatal inter-
" courfe about three weeks without
" any interruption, and as I had
" never heard from, or feen Can-
" taria, but in public places, where
" he never fpoke to me, I had not
" the leaft apprehenfions of him;
" but he was not fo idle as I
" imagined. Difmiffion from the
" office of *Cicifleo*, is one of the
" greateft indignities, that can be
" offered; and this haughty young
" Nobleman was refolved to be
" amply revenged of me. For this
" purpofe he fet watches upon my
" every motion, and as he knew
               " almoft

" almoft every place where Count
" Valeria and I vifited, there was
" not an action or an expreffion of
" mine that he was not acquainted
" with, except the place of private
" meeting with Lord K————,
" and that too he unfortunately dif-
" covered, but by what means I
" know not nor ever could learn;
" and the confequences removed all
" poffibility of enquiring.

" Lord K———— was one
" night fomewhat later in his ap-
" pointment than ufual, which gave
" me the utmoft uneafinefs. I had
" waited for him near half an hour,
" when my anxiety led me to look
" out of the window to fee for him,
" and although it was quite dark,

I 5 " I perceived

" I perceived a man walking feveral
" times by the houfe we were in;
" and from circumftances which I
" now recollect, I have fome reafon
" to conclude, that my woman knew
" it was Cantaria, tho' cloaked and
" mafqued. But we had not been
" long at the window before I per-
" ceived Lord K——— approach,
" who was likewife difguifed, and
" when he came within a few paces
" of the houfe, the perfon we before
" obferved walking fuddenly drew
" his fword, and made a dreadful
" pufh at him, which I thought
" went quite through his body, upon
" which I cried out, Murder! and
" inftantly fainted. and in that
" fituation I remained, infenfible and
" lifelefs, till I found myfelf re-
                    " covered,

" covered, and in the arms of Lord
" K————.

" As soon as I was sufficiently re-
" covered, my Lord informed me,
" that it was the villain Cantara,
" that had attempted to affassinate
" him, and had wounded him, but
" that he had received the reward
" of his barbarity, and was then
" lying in another apartment, he
" feared, expiring, that therefore
" there was not a moment to be
" loft, that as to me he would not
" part with me at the peril of his
" life, and that as the death of
" Cantara would be instantly found
" out, so the cause of it and our
" intercourse would be likewise made
" public : he therefore conjured me,
I 6   " that

" that moment, to fly with him out
" of the Venetian territories. At
" this inftant a fervant of my Lord's,
" who always attended at thefe
" apartments, and to whom he had
" given Cantaria in care, entered the
" room, and in the utmoft confufion
" told us, that he was dead. This
" gave us all a frefh alarm, and I
" was fo perfectly petrified with
" terror, grief and aftonifhment,
" that I was incapable of moving
" or fpeaking: therefore my Lord
" ordered his fervant to wrap me
" in his cloak, and carry me in his
" arms, until we could get a car-
" riage, and taking hold of my
" woman himfelf, we quitted this
" fatal houfe, and went through
" feveral dark ftreets and paffages,
" before

3

" before we durſt ſtop or call foi a
" coach   We at length got one,
" and drove to the utmoſt limits
" of the city, near the harbour,
" when my Lord ordered his ſervant
" to go directly in queſt of the
" Captain of an Engliſh ſhip, whom
" he had formerly known and ſailed
" with.   The ſervant returned in
" a few minutes with the Captain,
" and in leſs than a quarter of
" an hour we were aboard his
" ſhip.

" Lord K——— acquainted
" the Captain, whoſe name was
" Wilſon, with what had happened
" reſpecting Cantaria; and ſeeing
" me with him, and knowing his
" Lordſhip's general character, he
" eaſily

" eafily guefied the reft. And al-
" though he had not finifhed half
" his bufinefs at Venice, he im-
" mediately agreed to go with us
" to Genoa, and we fet fail ac-
" cordingly.

" After we had been fome time on
" board, and every thing was fettled
" for failing, my Lord afked the
" Captain if he had a furgeon on
" board, and being anfwered in the
" affirmative, he defired he would
" fend him into the cabbin, as
" he had received a little hurt
" in his arm. When the furgeon
" came and undreffed his arm,
" which was tied up with two or
" three handkerchefs to ftop the
" blood, he found his Lordfhip had
                    " received

" received a terrible wound in his
" left arm, and had loft a vaft
" quantity of blood, which his
" cloak prevented our feeing before.
" The furgeon immediately dreffed
" it, and my Lord made nothing
" of it. For my own part, from
" the moment I faw Cantaria's
" fword, to that inftant, I was per-
" fectly infenfible of every thing that
" paffed, and I had no more thought
" of going aboard fhip, and for
" ever quitting my parents, huf-
" band and friends, than if no fuch
" people ever exifted; but tacitly
" fubmitted to every thing my Lord
" did and ordered.

CHAP. XX.

" NOtwithstanding my Lord suf-
" fered much pain for several
" days we were at sea, he used every
" means in his power to comfort
" and entertain me, and my anxiety
" for his health engaged my atten-
" tion so much, that I did not then
" feel those severe reflections, which
" have since tortured me, for being
" the cause of so much distraction
" as I knew my unhappy conduct
" had occasioned, and the inexpres-
" sible grief it would give to my
" parents and husband. In short, I
" was so entirely devoted to this
" bewitching Lord, that I bore all
" those dreadful calamities with a
" resolution

" refolut.on and refignation, that
" both furprized and charmed him,
" and which he returned with the
" utmoft tendernefs, love and re-
" fpect; and after a very agreeable
" voyage we arrived fafe at Genoa,
" out of fear and apprehenfion.

" We ftaid at Genoa but a few
" days, until my Lord's wound was
" tolerably well, and to purchafe
" fome neceffaries both for myfelf
" and my woman, as we had not,
" during the paffage, a fingle change
" of either cloaths or linen; nor
" had my Lord any, but as he bor-
" rowed a fhirt from the Captain,
" who behaved to us with all pof-
" fible refpect, and entertained us
" in the very beft manner he was
                              " capable.

" capable   Lord K——— was
" here also under further obligations
" to Captain Wilfon, for he had no
" money, nor had he any Letters
" of credit on Genoa, but as foon
" as the Captain made known who
" he was, feveral gentlemen and
" merchants offered to advance what-
" ever fum his Lordfhip wanted.
" He accordingly took what was
" neceffary to carry him to Lyons,
" for which he gave bills on his
" banker at Paris, and made a
" prefent to Captain Wilfon of five
" hundred guineas, and fifty more
" to be divided amongft the fhip's
" crew.

" Having purchafed what necef-
" faries we wanted, we fet out from
" Genoa,

" Genoa for Turin My Lord and
" I travelled in one chaife, and his
" fervant and my woman in another,
" and we arrived at Turin the
" fecond dry. But the weather was
" fo intenfely cold in travelling over
" this mountainous country, that
" my Lord fuffered much in his
" arm, and I was almoft froze to
" death, tho' we were wrapt up in
" furr all over. We therefore re-
" mained at Turin for fome days;
" and my Lord wrote to Venice,
" and ordered his fervants to meet
" him with his baggage at Lyons,
" as foon as poffible.

" During our ftay at Turin, my
" Lord met with two Englifh
" Noblemen of his acquaintance in
" their

" their way to Venice and Naples,
" to whom he communicated our
" adventure, and as he was con-
" vinced, that the death of Cantaria
" and my elopement would make
" much noise in the republick, and
" would be juftly imputed to him,
" he requefted thefe Noblemen to
" reprefent the affair in it's true
" light, and clear his Lordfhip of
" the charge of having killed that
" unfortunate man, in any unfair
" or ungenerous manner, but in
" defence of his own life, when the
" other intended to affaffinate him.
" And with refpect to me, he en-
" treated his friends would wait on
" my parents and acquaint them,
" that they had feen me at Turin,
" in our way to Ireland, where his
                              " Lordfhip

" Lordſhip declared he would do
" every thing in his power to render
" me happy, but that after what
" had happened, it could not be
" expected I ſhould ever return to
" Venice: all which his noble friends
" promiſed to perform, and to ac-
" quaint his Lordſhip of what had
" paſſed, in a letter directed to his
" bankers at Paris.

" Theſe points ſettled, we ſet out
" from Turin to paſs the Alps,
" which I had often heard of, but
" never before approached; and in-
" deed it is impoſſible to entertain
" any juſt idea of them, without
" viewing and paſſing them.   The
" fiſt day's journey from Turin is
" to a place called Novaleſſe,
                    " through

" through a very fine country,
" which, at another feafon of the
" year, would have afforded us in-
" finite delight, from the variety of
" fruits, and charming plantations
" with which it abounds, and which
" my Lord affured me were equal
" to any to be found in any other
" part of Italy; but it was now in
" the month of December, and the
" whole country covered over with
" fnow and intenfely cold.

" The fecond day we began to
" afcend the famous mount Cenis,
" which is by much the higheft of
" all thofe wonderful mountains.
" At the bottom of this tremendous
" Alp, our chaifes were taken to
" pieces, and with our baggage put
                              " upon

" upon a number of mules, who
" climb up thofe otherwife inaccef-
" fible rocks, with a ftability and
" dexterity that would amaze you.
" We were all over wrapt up in
" furrs, and put into little feats or
" chairs of twifted rods, fixed upon
" poles, like thofe ufed here in
" fedan chairs, and in that manner
" were carried upon men's fhoulders;
" and although we fet out at day
" break in the morning, it was quite
" dark before we got to the bottom
" on the other fide of this one
" mountain, in croffing which I
" thought I fhould have been froze
" to death; nor fhould I have been
" able to ftand it, if we had not
" ftopt on the very fummit of the
" mountain, on which there is a
                                " plain

" plain of some miles over, and a
" very large lake filled with the
" finest trout in the world. Here
" there is a wretched cottage, where
" persons of all ranks and degrees,
" who travel this way, are obliged
" to stop for some refreshment, and
" it is the only place that any can be
" had during a whole day's severe
" journey.

" My Lord assured me, that when
" he passed this place in the summer
" before, he was highly delighted
" on this plain; that he had fished
" upon the lake, and never beheld
" a more delightful prospect: but
" it was now all over covered with
" snow many yards deep, and froze
" so hard, that the mules travelled
" on

" on it with great fafety. And I
" cannot help owning, that this
" amazing profpect of mountains,
" which are never free from fnow,
" the immenfe clouds which hung
" fufpended for feveral miles below
" our feet, and the dreadful cafcades
" of water rolling down the ftupen-
" dous rocks, with a noife that can
" be heard for feveral miles, ren-
" dered the whole fcene, if I may
" be allowed the expreffion — hor-
" ribly delightful.

" Three whole days we travelled
" through thefe mountains, with
" wretched accommodations of every
" fort, although there were two
" couriers went poft conftantly be-
" fore us, to provide provifions and

K   " horfes.

" horfes. We at laft arrived at
" Pont Beauvoifin, the frontier town
" of France; which, by a fmall
" bridge, divides that kingdom from
" the dominions of Savoy. And
" the fourth night we got into
" Lyons, to my great comfort and
" fatisfaction.

" We remained at Lyons for
" feveral days, waiting for my
" Lord's retinue and baggage, which
" at length arrived by the way of
" Marfeilles. Our time was here
" very agreeably fpent, in viewing
" the curiofities of the place, and the
" greateft filk manufactures in the
" world, with an immenfe quantity
" of which, the richeft and moft
" beautiful I had ever feen, my
" Lord

" Lord filled feveral chefts for my
" ufe, which I took with me to
" Paris, and had them there made
" in the moft elegant and fafhionable
" tafte, and in the purchafe of
" thefe and other neceffaries, with
" fome diamonds and trinkets, my
" Lord expended feveral thoufand
" pounds, and gave me in every
" other refpect the higheft proofs of
" his generofity, love and refpect;
" fo that I began to refume my for-
" mer tranquillity, and enjoy the
" higheft happinefs in his company
" and converfation, nor was he
" hardly ever an hour abfent from
" me.

" After a month's ftay at Paris,
" my Lord received letters from his
K 2 " friends

" friends whom he had parted with
" at Turin, congratulating him on
" his escape from Venice, and in-
" forming him, that he had not
" sailed half an hour before the
" whole city was in an uproar, and
" that if he had been taken with
" me, it would have been impossible
" to have saved his life, the power
" and resentment both of my father
" and husband, and that of the Can-
" taria family, were so great—that
" Count Valeria threatened to pursue
" us even to Ireland; and they
" advised my Lord by all means
" not to stay at Paris, as they
" doubted not but some villains
" would be there employed to assas-
" sinate him, and perhaps seize me.
" This account alarmed me so
                              " much,

" much, that I would not fleep
" another night in Paris for a king-
" dom, and I had influence enough
" over my Lord to prevail with him
" to fet out that very night, and
" the third day we arrived fafe at
" Dover, where I was fatisfied we
" were out of all danger.

C H A P. XXI

" SOME few nights after our
" arrival in London, Lord
" K——— took me to the play,
" where, in the very next box, I
" met with the Venetian Ambaſ-
" ſador, who was a near relation of
" mine, and particularly intimate
" with me and all my family. He
" was as much aſtoniſhed at ſeeing
" me, as I was terrified and alarmed
" at ſeeing him ; for I doubted not
" but he had heard of my elope-
" ment, and the death of Lord
" Cantaria, to whom he was alſo
" related. Nor was I deceived in
" that opinion ; for, after a very
" cold ſalute, I could perceive he
" was

" was prodigioufly uneafy, and after
" fome time retired, which I con-
" cluded was to give orders to have
" me watched, and to find out my
" refidence. This new alarm fo
" terrified me, that I had like to
" have fainted. My Lord obferved
" my diftrefs, and enquiring the
" caufe, I informed him of my
" fufpicions, and begged he would
" permit me to leave the houfe di-
" rectly, which, in regard to me,
" he complied with ; and having
" conducted me out at a private
" door, put me into a chair without
" any attendants but himfelf, and
" ordered the chairmen to ftop at a
" certain ftreet which he mentioned,
" but not at the place of our re-
" fidence.

K 4 " We

" We had not gone far, when
" my Lord called a hackney coach,
" which we both got into and went
" home; and, by this caution,
" eluded any enquiry the Ambaf-
" fador might have made after me:
" nor could my Lord ever after-
" wards, during our ftay in London,
" prevail with me to go into any
" public place or meeting, which
" very much difconcerted him, as
" he intended to have fpent the re-
" mainder of the winter in England.
" But this adventure, and my refo-
" lution not to appear any more
" in public, determined him to fet
" out for Ireland, and we arrived at
" Dublin in a few days afterwards.

" It

" It had been reported to feveral
" of my Lord's friends in that king-
" dom, that he had been murdered
" at Venice, and they had received
" a very imperfect account of our
" adventure there; but his fudden
" and unexpected appearance gave
" fo much joy and fatisfaction, that
" for feveral days he was not per-
" mitted to be one moment alone.
" His houfe was perpetually filled
" with perfons of the firft diftinction,.
" who flew to congratulate his Lord-
" fhip on his fafe arrival, for I need
" not tell you how much and how
" univerfally he was beloved and
" refpected. We remained near
" three months in Dublin, and I
" was entertained by his Lordfhip
" and all his friends (except ladies,)

" with the fame refpect and dif-
" tinction, as if I had been married
" to him, and he had given pofitive
" directions to all his fervants and
" domefticks to treat and obey me
" as fuch; fo that I was as happy
" as the nature of my fituation
" would admit, and I believe, that,
" during that period, his Lordfhip
" was never guilty of any infidelity
" to me."

" Some time in May following he
" took me to Rockingham, which
" I need not defcribe to you. I
" was charmed with this delightful
" place, and as I had centered all
" my happinefs in my Lord's pre-
" fence and company, and as I en-
" joyed much more of it there, than
" I could

" I could poſſibly do in town, I
" grew perfectly pleaſed with my
" ſituation, and I ſoon diſcovered
" that I was pregnant.

   " This event ſo delighted my
" Lord, that he, if poſſible, doubled
" his aſſiduity to pleaſe and indulge
" me in every thing.   You have
" ſeen the manner he lived in at
" this enchanting ſeat, and have
" experienced his power to pleaſe.
" In ſhort, every thing about me
" was a perfect paradiſe, and all
" devoted to my pleaſures.   In this
" delightful manner we paſſed the
" ſummer, and as the time of my
" delivery drew near, we repaired
" to town in October; and, about
" the middle of November, I was

" mother

" mother of one of the fineſt boys
" in the univerſe. My Lord was
" all tranſport, and every prepara-
" tion was made and attendance
" given, ſuited to a perſon of the
" firſt rank and diſtinction; and he
" had the child called Robert, after
" his own chriſtian name.

" A nurſe was, at my particular
" deſire, taken into the houſe, and
" my whole attention was engroſſed
" by my lovely boy, nor was my
" Lord leſs fond of him, which
" rendered me entirely happy; when
" a curſed adventure interfered, that
" blaſted all my hope of future
" happineſs and repoſe. My Lord
" was taken in bed with the honour-
" able Mrs. G———, a near rela-
" tion

" tion of his own, and the wife of
" a perfon of the very firft rank and
" family in the kingdom. The
" manner, in which they were dif-
" covered, rendered it impoffible to
" keep the affair fecret. It was
" fpread all over the city in a few
" days, and a profecution was com-
" menced againft my Lord by the
" hufband; whilft the Lady was
" immediately put into a fhip in the
" harbour by her own family, carried
" over to France, and there immured
" in a cloifter, where fhe remains
" to this day. And my Lord, at
" the requeft and by the perfuafion
" of many of his friends, retired
" into the country, until the con-
" fufion, which this fhameful amour
" had produced, fhould be blown
" over.

" I need not mention to you, nor
" indeed can I, the tortures I felt
" on this occafion. I became fran-
" tic, and upbraided my Lord for
" his infidelity, and the infult he
" had offered to me, in terms that
" were, I own, rather too violent,
" and both furprized and offended
" him; for you know with what
" impatience he could hear any of
" his faults, or remonftrance againft
" them. We had not been long in
" the country before we quarreled
" and became fo uneafy, that he
" ordered feparate beds, and fhortly
" after openly avowed his incon-
" ftancy by keeping wenches in the
" very houfe with me. On reflec-
" tion, I think it but juftice to his
" Lordfhip's memory to own I was
" much

" much to blame on this occafion ;
" that my behaviour to him was too
" violent and aggravating; and that
" if I had prefeived more modeia-
" tion and difcretion, he never would
" have treated me with that dif-
" iefpect and indifference, which I
" ever afterwards fo fatally expe-
" rienced.   For fome time I was
" really out of my fenfes; but my
" youth and inexperience, joined
" to the violence of my love and
" attachment to him, blinded my
" underftanding, and I gave entire
" fway to my paffions without once
" reflecting on the confequences.

" The meafure of my misfortunes
" was not however yet full, tho'
" I thought myfelf as miferable as
" any

" any human wretch could be
" made. My dear boy was taken
" with that cruel diftemper called
" the fmall pox, and died in a
" few days. I fhall not attempt
" to defcribe my forrows on that
" occafion, nor did I ever fee my
" Lord fo much affected. He was
" really grieved, and for fome days
" would not fee any company. For
" a whole week I had never fpoke
" to him or feen him, but remained
" in my own apartments, where I
" wept myfelf into a perfect ftupe-
" faction, regardlefs of every thing
" that furrounded me.

CHAP. XXII.

" FROM this lethargy I was
" roufed by the arrival of a
" number of my Lord's moft riotous
" and debauched companions, who
" had been previoufly engaged to
" come down to hunt with him;
" and as nothing could long affect
" his gay fpirits, he foon returned
" to his ufual exceffes of drinking
" and debaucheries of every fort;
" fo that the houfe became a per-
" fect brothel. It is true, he never
" permitted any of his abandoned
" company to come near or difturb
" me. I had a fet of the beft a-
" partments in the houfe, appointed
" for my fepaiate ufe, the moft
　　　　　" remote

" remote from the scene of riot and
" intoxication, and my Lord regu-
" larly every morning paid me a
" visit, behaved to me with the
" higheft respect, and gave strict
" orders for my being attended and
" furnished with every thing I
" desired; and in this situation
" we continued to live for several
" months.

" My Lord saw, and was touched
" with my misfortunes. He can-
" didly confessed he had treated me
" ill, but that he could not account
" for the ficklenefs of his temper
" and extravagant desires; and very
" generously offered to accompany
" me to any part of Europe I should
" chuse for my residence, and to
                              " settle

" fettle an annuity on me for life,
" that would enable me to live up
" to the height of my ambition—
" all which I refufed I was ap-
" prehenfive, that, if I went to any
" other part of Europe out of his
" protection, my refidence would be
" found out by my hufband or pa-
" rents, and that they would by
" force carry me to Venice, which I
" dreaded much more than death
" itfelf. I was an entire ftranger
" both in England and Ireland, and
" did not know where or to whom
" I fhould remove, and was de-
" lighted with the fituation I was
" then in. I therefore requefted his
" Lordfhip would permit me to
" continue at Rockingham, and af-
" fured him I would not prefume
" to

" to interrupt his pleasures or pur-
" suits, in what I saw he could not
" be restrained from.

" In this melancholy situation I
" had remained upwards of three
" years, when you arrived at Rock-
" ingham; and in the course of
" that time, it is incredible to think
" what a number of unhappy young
" creatures were daily sacrificed to
" the lust and passions of this
" strange, extravagant Lord, and
" his more abandoned, profligate
" companions; tho' there were but
" few of them of any note or family,
" nor did I ever keep company
" with any of them, but two or
" three, who, I knew, were persons
" of some condition, and had been
                    " seduced

" feduced to this manfion of de-
" ftruction, before your arrival;
" and from the moment I faw you,
" I was prejudiced in your favour,
" and felt feverely for the ruin,
" which I knew would be brought
" upon you by your love for my
" Lord. On his return from England
" after the marriage of Mifs J——,
" he expreffed to me his concern
" for you, and the apprehenfions
" he was under that fome accident
" had happened to you, and moft
" of all that no fettlement or pro-
" vifion had been made for you;
" and added, that left fome fatal
" accident fhould prevent his pro-
" viding for me in future, he in-
" fifted I fhould then accept of a
" deed of annuity of 600 l. a year,

4   " payable

" payable half yearly during my
" life, together with a legacy of
" 1000 l. payable in one month
" after his death, if I ſhould ſurvive
" him.

CHAP. XXIII.

"AS soon as thefe matters were
" fettled, he gave orders that
" every thing fhould be got ready
" for his journey to Vienna, and
" from thence to the Court of
" Ruffia, but a few days before
" he was to fet out, he was taken
" with an apoplexy, and in one
" moment depiived of the power of
" fpeech and the ufe of all his
" limbs, but with proper care he
" was iecovered in a fhort time.
" The fortitude and refignation,
" with which he bore this dreadful
" fhock, aftonifhed me and every
" perfon prefent. He ordered every
" body out of the room, and with

" an

" an affection and tenderneſs, that
" overwhelm'd me with grief, de-
" ſired I would let him know, if
" there was any thing I deſired
" ſhould be done for me, or added
" to the proviſion already made for
" me. ' I know,' continued his
" Lordſhip, ' that the ſhock I have
' had is the ſignal for my diſſolu-
' tion ; and I don't know any crime
' I have been guilty of, that weighs
' ſo heavy upon my mind, as ſedu-
' cing a Lady of your rank, beauty,
' and fortune, from your elevated
' ſtation in life , and the thought
' of leaving you here, friendleſs and
' forſaken, at this moment renders
' me miſerable.' " This kind con-
" cern for me, and the manner in
" which he expreſſed it, more than
" recompenſed

" recompenfed all my former fuf-
" ferings. I funk before him, dif-
" folved in tears, love and grati-
" tude; and affured him I was
" amply provided for, and had not
" a wifh for any more worldly
" riches; but begged of him to
" compofe himfelf, and ardently
" prayed that the hour of his death
" might be many—many years dif-
" tant. ' My dear Valeria!' re-
" plied his Lordfhip, ' that cannot
' be; the life I have led, ever fince
' I was fixteen, will not, in the na-
' ture of things, permit it; and
' for fome time I have perceived
' violent fymptoms of what has now
' happened, and, I am fure, will
' fhortly return, and end all my
' enjoyments in this life. 'Tis a

L   ' kind

‘ kind of death I am pleafed with ;
‘ and as I have already enjoyed more
‘ than one man's fhare of worldly
‘ pleafures, I am perfectly willing
‘ to refign   My friends have long
‘ endeavoured to perfuade me to
‘ marry, as well to furnifh an heir
‘ to my title and eftate, as to re-
‘ claim me from that extravagance
‘ in purfuit of your fex, which I
‘ flatter myfelf has been my only
‘ foible, and has irrefiftibly hurried
‘ me into thofe many dangers, ex-
‘ ceffes and crimes, that I now
‘ fincerely repent of, but I could
‘ not, nor would not marry any
‘ woman that I did not entirely love,
‘ and I was too well acquainted
‘ with my own unhappy temper and
‘ conftitution, not to be convinced,

                        ‘ I fhould

' I fhould make her miferable. I
' therefore declined every overture
' of that nature that was made to
' me, which at this moment gives
' me the greateft pleafure and com-
' fort I am capable of receiving.
" His Lordfhip concluded with ad-
" vifing me to go into the fouth of
" France, and place myfelf in fome
" genteel convent, until I fhould
" hear from my parents, or fome
" other event might enable me to
" return to my native country.

" His Lordfhip then called in
" Mr. K——, his younger brother,
" in whofe favour he had made his
" will, and conjured him, in the
" moft pathetic manner, to fhew me
" every act of tendernefs and friend-

" fhip

" fhip in his power; and that in
" cafe he fhould be able to difcover
" you, he fhould in the like manner
" amply provide for and befriend
" you—which Mr. K——— pro-
" mifed faithfully to perform. My
" Lord then acquainted his brother,
" that he had advanced feveral fums
" of money to feveral needy gen-
" tlemen, his friends and compa-
" nions, which they would not
" accept of, but as borrowed from
" him, and for which they had
" given him bonds, notes, &c.;
" that he was convinced many of
" them were prejudiced in their
" circumftances from many extra-
" vagancies, which they had com-
" mitted in his company, and which
" their fortunes could not afford;
                                " and

" and that at the time he advanced
" the money, for which he received
" their bonds, he never intended to
" demand any payment of them.
" He therefore defired they fhould
" be all brought to him, and he in-
" ftantly put the whole bundle into
" the fire. After this he was per-
" fectly chearful, and refumed his
" former vivacity, which he enjoyed
" for feven days, till at laft he was
" feized with a fecond fit, which
" put an end to his life.

" Notwithftanding this noble
" Lord's innumerable follies, I don't
" believe there ever was a man's
" death fo univerfally lamented, by
" all ranks and degrees of people.
" The moment he died, all his

L 3 " vices

" vices died with him, and were
" utterly forgot; but his unexam-
" pled benevolence, generofity and
" hofpitality, were all gratefully
" remembered and applauded; and
" the cries and lamentations of
" many hundreds of his poor
" tenants, labourers and fervants,
" were heard and continued for
" feveral days through all parts of
" the country, and followed him to
" his grave. And I was affured,
" that fuch a funeral was never
" feen in that country, that feveral
" thoufands of gentlemen and ladies
" attended at his interment from
" all parts of the kingdom, to
" teftify their refpect and efteem for
" the memory of their noble friend.

" After

" After his interment, as foon as
" decency would permit, I acquainted
" Mr. K—— with my defire of
" fulfilling his Lordfhip's directions,
" in retiring to France, which he
" readily agreed to; and imme-
" diately gave me an order on his
" banker in Dublin, for the 1000 l.
" his brother had bequeathed me,
" with directions to draw half
" yearly for my annuity. He then
" prefented me with a valuable ring,
" as a token of his refpect for me,
" and ordered his own poft chaife,
" horfes and fervants, to attend me
" to Dublin. I have been but a
" few days in London in my way
" to France, where if my dear Mifs
" Faulkner will accompany me,
" fhe fhall with the greateft plea-

L 4 " fure

" fure fhare my little fortune, and
" I think it enough to fupply us
" both with every thing we can
" defire, in that part of the world."

Here Lady Valeria ended her
melancholy hiftory, with which Mifs
Faulkner was equally affected and
delighted; and they mutually con-
doled with each other, and lamented
the death of their beloved Lord
K————; and after Mifs Faulkner had returned fuitable acknowledgements for the trouble Lady
Valeria had taken to oblige her,
and for the generous and polite
offer fhe had made to her, which
fhe was forced to decline on account
of her very bad ftate of health,
they

they parted with affurances of feeing and entertaining each other, as often as poffible, during Lady Valeria's fhort ftay in London.

C H A P. XXIV.

THERE is no greater relief to a suffering mind, than a companion in our afflictions. The misfortunes of Lady Valeria leffened those of Mifs Faulkner, and, by the fenfible advice and coidial friend-fhip of that lady, fhe began to re-cover her ftrength and fpuits. They were almoft conftantly together, and as Lady Valeria was an excellent judge of mufick, and knew Mifs Faulkner's elegant tafte and ad-mirable performance in that art, and hearing of the extravagant falaries given to all the eminent performeis in our public entertainments, fhe advifed her to practife and ftudy it

with

with some attention, and that she could not fail of getting a very genteel income by it.

Lady Valeria having settled what business she had to do in London, and despairing of getting Miss Faulkner to go with her into France, set out for Dover, whither Miss Faulkner attended her, accompanied by Mis. Preston, in a post chaise, and the next day they parted, with mutual assurances of the most inviolable friendship and constant correspondence by letters.

On her return to London, our heroine began seriously to consider her situation. She knew, that the small fortune she had would not be

L 6   sufficient

fufficient to fupport her for any length
of time, in a life of idlenefs; and
the opinion and advice of Lady
Valeria had great weight with her.
She therefore fold the moft valuable
part of her jewels, and fome cloaths,
which fhe thought unfit for her ufe;
and the produce of thefe, with the
remainder of her cafh which fhe
had not fpent, amounted to upwards of 600 l. which, with the
affiftance of Mrs. Prefton, fhe laid
out in the purchafe of bank ftock.
She then bought a harpfichord, and
began to practice and ftudy with the
utmoft diligence: . and having communicated her defign of appearing
in public to Mrs. Prefton, that gentlewoman brought one of the firft
performers and beft judges to hear

her

her play and fing. Mr. L—— was charmed with her, and being then proprietor of Mary le Bonne gardens, immediately engaged her at a very genteel falary; and fhe made her firft public appearance there that very fummer.

Never was any new performer fo applauded, or fo much encouraged as Mifs Faulkner. Her voice and tafte for mufick were greatly admired; but the elegance of her perfon, her modeft deportment, and the natural fweetnefs of her temper and her affability, procured her univerfal efteem and refpect; and every night the gardens were crowded with the genteeleft company, to hear and fee this admirable young lady.

We

We muſt ſuppoſe the gentlemen, moſt famous for gallantry and intrigue, were not idle on this new acquiſition to their pleaſures : for, however unreaſonable or unjuſt it may be deemed, by much the majority of our nobility and gentlemen of fortune immediately conclude, that any young woman, who makes her appearance on the ſtage, or any of the other public places of entertainment, becomes their lawful prize; and that they have a right to treat and inſult her with their ſcandalous propoſals for debauching and keeping, though ſhe is perfectly modeſt and averſe to ſuch ſentiments. This is a real hardſhip on thoſe young ladies, whoſe merit, youth, and ſex, intitle them

to

to the public encouragement and protection; and although neceffity may oblige them to enter into that ftate of life for their fupport, and to avoid proftitution, it by no means juftifies the cruelty or infolence of thofe unthinking fools of fafhion, who are hourly peftering them with their loathfome and infipid addreffes and propofals.

Mifs Faulkner fuffered prodigioufly from this fhameful cuftom. Many confiderable propofals and offers of fettlement were made to her, which fhe rejected with a refentment and difdain, that did her no lefs honour, than it abafhed and mortified the *ninny hammers* that made them;

them, and, for that feafon, fhe efcaped without the fmalleft cenfure on her conduct, and with the higheft public applaufe.

CHAP. XXV.

IN the winter it was expected and agreed on, that she should make her appearance on Covent Garden theatre, but amongst the number of her admirers was one Mr. D————, a young gentleman of very genteel appearance and polite address.   He used every possible means of getting acquainted with her, and at last effected it through Mrs. Preston, in whose house Miss Faulkner still continued to board and lodge.   Mr. D———— assured Mrs. Preston, that his intentions respecting Miss Faulkner were strictly honourable, and that he was a gentleman of an independant fortune;

that

that her lodger had made the deepeſt impreſſion on his heart, and that, if ſhe would countenance and encourage his addreſſes, he would amply reward her. Mrs. Preſton aſſured him, that, if his deſigns were honourable, and his addreſſes agreeable to Miſs Faulkner, ſhe would do him any ſervice in her power; and the next morning engaged him to breakfaſt with herſelf and our heroine.

Mr. D———— had before ſeveral times occaſionally ſpoke to Miſs Faulkner in publick, merely as a ſinger, and to compliment her on her performance. She immediately recollected him, and being aſſured by Mrs. Preſton, that his addreſſes were perfectly honourable, ſhe received

ceived him with her usual politeness
and civility; and as soon as breakfast
was finished, and Mrs. Preston withdrawn, Mr. D————— made a formal declaration of his passion: that
he had long wished for an opportunity of assuring her his intentions
were sincere and honourable; that
his fortune, though not abundant,
was competent and independant;
and that if she would condescend
to think favourably of him, he
would esteem himself extremely
honoured in her acceptance of his
hand and fortune. He added, that
he was no stranger either to her
disagreeable situation, or the nau-
seous proposals which were every
day made to her, and she had
nobly refused, that these refusals
encreased

encreafed his efteem for her, and
juftified the impreffion which her
beauty had firft made upon him;
that when it fhould be known fhe
was married to a gentleman, her
troublefome fuitors would defift from
their ungenerous and mean purfuits,
but that whilft fhe continued fingle,
fhe muft not expect any refpite from
their importunities.

Mifs Faulkner, with great attention, heard the whole of Mr.
D————'s declaration, and returned him fuitable compliments for
his kind intentions and favourable
opinion of her; but affured him,
that fhe did not entertain the leaft
thoughts about matrimony, and were
fhe but free from thofe fulfome and
disagreeable

difagreeable follicitations he had mentioned, fhe fhould be extremely well contented with her fituation: that if any thing could perfuade her to alter her condition, it would be the very motives he had mentioned; but that at prefent fhe could not think of it. Mr. D——— however obtained her permiffion to repeat his vifits, and after expreffing his hopes, that his future conduct would procure him fome part of her efteem, he took a moft refpectful leave of her for that time; but more than ever in love and charmed with her good fenfe and elegant behaviour.

Although courtfhip is a pleafing fubject, we fhall not here dwell longer

upon

upon it, let it fuffice, that Mr. D——— was fo affiduous in his addreffes, and rendered himfelf fo very agreeable to Mifs Faulkner, that, at the end of three months, fhe confented to give him her hand, and they were married in as private a manner as poffible.

CHAP. XXVI.

MR. D——— was so very generous in his addresses to Miss Faulkner, that, during the whole time of their courtship, he never once enquired into her circumstances or fortune; and her own integrity, generosity and inexperience, prevented her ever entertaining a thought on that subject, with respect to his circumstances. She really liked him, and considered herself as highly honoured and obliged in the generosity of a gentleman, of his appearance and independence, marrying her in the situation of life she was in; and therefore never suspected the least impoſition;

impofition; and in a few days after
their marriage fhe acquainted him,
that fhe had in the funds 600 l. to
difpofe of as he thought proper.

This was a circumftance, that
Mr. D———— was before well
acquainted with, and in reality was
the *load-ftone* that attracted all his
affections to the unfufpecting Mifs
Faulkner. It is true, he once had
a fmall fortune, which was entirely
confumed in gaming and other follies, and he was now reduced to
the moft defperate circumftances, and
therefore feized this 600 l. as the
only means to keep him from a
prifon and immediate poverty.
Neverthelefs he kept up appearances
with his wife, and, after he had got

this

this money, they lived fome time in great content and tranquillity, and fhe was perfectly happy in her choice.

Their fun fhine did not, however, long continue. Mr D————— took to his old trade of gaming, and affociating with a fet of villains, who had before cheated him out of his fortune, they in a few months ftript him of every fhilling of his laft acquifition. This made him defperate, and he plunged himfelf into every fort of debauch and ex- cefs. He threw off every appear- ance of love and refpect for his wife, and by degrees ftript her of even her wearing apparel, and every neceffary fhe had about her perfon;

M   and

and, to compleat the horror of her
mifery, he gave her the foul diftemper, and then abfconded both
from her and his creditors, to avoid
that prifon from which fhe had before
redeen ed him.

It would but too much affect a
fympathizing heart, to defcribe what
our unfortunate heroine fuffered on
this occafion. She was reduced to
the moft deplorable circumftances,
without a fecond change of apparel,
or any friend on earth to affift or
relieve her, but her greateft misfortune was the dreadful diftemper,
which fhe laboured under for fome
time, before fhe knew or ever fufpected the caufe Mrs. Prefton
firft difcovered it, and as fhe was

3   principally

principally the means of this fatal connection with Mr. D————, she was indeed deeply afflicted. — She made immediate application to Mr. M————, a gentleman of her acquaintance, who, she knew, had a very great friendship for Miss Faulkner, as well before as after her marriage, and acquainted him with her unhappy situation and circumstances

Mr M———— had a heart abounding with compassion and benevolence, but his circumstances prevented his giving the immediate assistance, that his inclinations and this unfortunate lady's case required. He contributed what he could towards it; but was resolved to sol-

M 2 licit

licit and procure for her, what he was not able to do himſelf He was at that time very intimate with Lord H———, and knew, that his Lordſhip's heart and purſe were ever open to diſtreſſed merit.   To him therefore Mr M——— immediately applied, and related ſo much as he knew of our heroine's hiſtory and diſtreſſes, in ſo pathetic and moving a manner, that his Lordſhip inſtantly diſpatched him with a bank-note of 50 l. to our fair ſufferer, and deſired that a ſurgeon of the firſt eminence ſhould be foithwith employed, and every other atten-dance given for her immediate cure, all which he would chearfully pay.

Mr,

Mr M——— in raptures returned to Mrs. Prefton, and acquainted
her with his fuccefs Mrs Prefton
was no lefs overjoyed. but all that
fhe could fay, could not perfuade
Mr. M——— to approach the object of their mutual concern, left
he fhould abafh and confufe her.
He knew her delicacy and modefty
would be fhocked at his knowledge
of her condition, and therefore would
not go into her prefence, but giving
Mrs Prefton the bank note, he defired her to go and purchafe whatever
neceffaries were wanting; and went
directly himfelf to engage a furgeon.

Mifs Faulkner was an utter ftranger
to every thing that paffed upon this
occafion, nor had Mrs. Prefton fully

M 3 apprized.

apprized her of the dangerous fituation fhe was in, but as foon as the
furgeon came, after a proper confultation between Mr. M————, the
furgeon, and herfelf, for that purpofe, he was introduced to Mifs
Faulkner, as a furgeon of Mrs.
Prefton's acquaintance, who called
accidentally, and, as fhe was indif-
pofed, would prefcribe fomething
for her; and by degrees, the affair
was thus opened, until the furgeon
explained to her the neceffity of her
fubmitting to a regular cure. All
the misfortunes, that had ever before happened to her, were trifling
to what fhe felt, on this information
of the nature of her diforder, and
fhe would have chearfully refigned
her life, rather than bear the infamy,
which

which she conceived the very name of this difeafe carried with it. She was, however, oblig d to fubmit, and, in a little time after, Mrs. Prefton informed her of the obligations fhe was under to Mr. M——, who had procured her fuch affiftance both of friends and money.

M 4

CHAP XXVII.

AT the expiration of two months
our fair fufferer was once more
re-eftablifhed in her health, but rendered extremely weak and delicate,
nor had fhe for fome time before,
or fince her illnefs, ever heard a
fyllable of Mr D————. The
furgeon, who attended her, reported
daily the progrefs of her cure to Mr.
M————, who conftantly reported
it to Lord H————, and when
fhe was perfectly recovered, his
Lordfhip fignified his intention to
Mr. M———— of vifiting his fair
friend, as foon as it was agreeable
to her.

Mr.

Mr. M—— immediately ac-
quainted Mifs Faulkner, (as we fhall
continue to call her) with his Lordfhip's intentions; and though her
gratitude obliged her to receive his
Lordfhip with every mark of refpect, fhe was fo overcome with
grief, confufion, and diftrefs, at the
caufe of this vifit, that fhe would
have given any confideration to avoid
the interview: but there was no alternative, and a day was accordingly fixed for his Lordfhip to vifit
her. Mr. M—— introduced his
Lordfhip, who, with his ufual affability and politenefs, requefted Mifs
Faulkner would favour him with
a difh of tea, and although our
heroine, as well as Mr. M——, feveral times attempted to introduce the

M 5 obliga-

obligations his Lordſhip had conferred, he politely evaded hearing
it, and ſhewed Mr. M——— that
it would be diſagreeable to him to
have it mentioned. His Lordſhip
was charmed with the behaviour
and ſenſibility of Miſs Faulkner;
and after tea, requeſted Mr. M———
would intercede with his fair friend
for the favour of a ſong, which ſhe
immediately conſented to. Lord
H——— is a perfect judge, and a
great admirer of muſick, and he
was now at once delighted and ſurprized. He had indeed heard of
this lady's inimitable voice and performance, but ſhe exceeded every
thing he had formed an idea of,
and he was ſenſibly ſtruck, as well
with the beauty and elegance of her
                                    perſon,

perſon, as with the raviſhing harmony of her voice.

Lord H——— took Mr. M——— home with him in his chariot, and aſſured him, that he had never felt more exquiſite delight than in the company of our heroine, that it was his firm purpoſe to put her above both want and temptation; and as an inſtance of his regard for her, he gave Mr M——— bank notes to the amount of 200 l. deſiring, he would immediately remove her from Mrs. Preſton's, and take proper lodgings, where he might ſee and viſit her, and that Miſs Faulkner ſhould furniſh herſelf with cloaths and other neceſſaries, with the remainder of the money.

M 6 For

For feveral months afterwards
his Lordfhip continued to vifit, and
fpent feveral moft delightful even-
ings with Mifs Faulkner, without
fhewing the leaft particular attachment to her, other than the ufual
compliments on her extraordinary
mufical abilities; and behaved to her
with fo much refpect and affability,
and at the fame time with fuch
generofity, tendernefs, and delicacy,
that fhe was entirely overcome with
gratitude and efteem for him, in fo
much that fhe perfectly adored him.
At length, his paffion for his fair
ward became too violent to be longer
reftrained. He with reluctance, but
with the greateft delicacy, opened
his mind to her, and if fhe did not
love his Lordfhip, as much as he
                                    defired,

defired, her gratitude and efteem for him put it out of her power to refufe him any thing he could requeft of her.

In fhort, the apprehenfion of being detected and feized by Mr. D———— feemed to be the only objection or obftacle to their union, and that Lord H———— undertook to remove His Lordfhip was then at the head of one of the moft confiderable offices under the crown, and had fuch diligent enquiry made after Mr. D————, that he with fome difficulty found him out, and after feverely reprimanding him for the infamy of his conduct and behaviour to his wife, his Lordfhip told him, that if he

would

would go to America, and engage
never to return to England to difturb or moleſt her, he would inſtantly furniſh him with a ſum of money
to carry him there, and provide him
with neceſſaries, and that he would
give him an employment worth
500l. a year, during his continuance in that place.

Mr D———— very clearly un-
derſtood his Lordſhip's intentions;
but this was too advantageous an
offer, for a man in his circumſtances to refuſe. He did not
therefore heſitate about accepting
the propoſal. his Lordſhip ſtrictly
fulfilled all his engagements, and
Mr. D———— embarked for America in leſs than a week after the
treaty was concluded.

C H A P. XXVIII.

AS foon as Lord H———— knew
that Mr D———————— was failed, he waited on our heroine with
the news, with which fhe was perfectly pleafed, and declared herfelf
entirely at his Lordfhip's difpofal;
upon which he took out of his pocket a paper, which he read to her,
whereby he had fettled 400 l. a year
upon her for life, payable to proper truftees, for her fole and feparate
ufe, independant of her hufband;
and fhe went home immediately to
his Lordfhip's houfe, but in the
character of goveinefs to two young
ladies, his daughters, and in that
fituation fhe remained, till her pregnancy,

nancy, in lefs than a year, made it neceffary fhe fhould retire into the country for fome time.

Lord H————'s love and efteem for our heroine every day encreafed, and her behaviour, sweetnefs of temper, and perpetual ftudy to pleafe and amufe him, juftly intitled her to his utmoft regards, nor were the young ladies, his daughters, lefs fond of her. After fhe was brought to bed in the country, fhe immediately returned to his Lordfhip's houfe in town, and the young ladies having before made fome progrefs in mufick, and having naturally a fine ear and tafte, Mifs Faulkner devoted her whole time and affiduity to their inftruction, till they became

the

the admiration of every body that heard them.

At the expiration of another year, Mifs Faulkner was obliged to retire a fecond time into the country, and was delivered of a fecond child, which was alfo fent to nurfe; and on her return to town, his Lordfhip was under a neceffity of taking a feparate houfe for her, the reafon whereof fhe did not then know, or enquire into, as his will was a law to her.

Lord H——— had been many years a widower, and his great generofity and benevolence always kept him in diftreffed circumftances; and as he was extremely refpected and beloved

beloved by almoſt all ranks of people, ſeveral of his friends adviſed him to marry ſome woman of large fortune, and thereby diſcharge the many incumbrances which devoured his eſtate, and enable him to live in that ſplendor which his rank and inclinations required. It was a long time before he could reſolve on this project, though he knew the expediency of it, and his ſtrong attachment to Miſs Faulkner was his greateſt difficulty. But neceſſity, and the perſuaſion of his friends at length prevailed; and he accordingly paid his addreſſes to a lady, that had been fixed upon, one of the greateſt fortunes in the kingdom. He met with every encouragement he could wiſh for; and after

a courtſhip of a few months, marriage articles were prepared, and a
day appointed for the celebration of
the nuptials.

This treaty, and every negotiation
relative thereto, was kept a profound ſecret from Miſs Faulkner;
nor did ſhe ever hear or ſuſpeét
any thing of it, till a few days before that fixed on for his Lordſhip's
marriage. The news almoſt diſtraét-
ed her; and ſhe was determined, if
poſſible, to prevent this union, on
which all her future welfare and
happineſs depended. She therefore
poſted into the country, for her two
children, and the very day before
Lord H——— was to be married,
ſhe got admittance into his Lordſhip's.

ship's houfe, when he leaft expected
to fee her, and falling proftrate before him, with a child in each hand,
fhe begged his Lordfhip to have pity
on her, and not defert heifelf and
thofe innocent babes In fhort, fhe
pleaded fo powerfully, and the com-
paffionate heart of her Lc   ʃ
fenfibly moved with her unfeignea
grief and diftrefs, that he was entirely fubdued; his regards for her
returned upon him with fuch irre-
fiftible tendernefs, that he raifed
her from her proftrate pofture,
embraced her, and declared that
to gain an empire, he would never
defert or forfake her. She was loft
in tranfport, and her teais only
expreffed her gratitude and her joy;
to complete which, his Lordfhip, in

her prefence, wrote a letter to the lady he was to be married to the next day, acquainting her, that fome infurmountable obftacles had intervened, which prevented the honour of the union fhe intended him and the whole negotiation was finally fet afide, to the aftonifhment and vexation of all his Lordfhip's friends, as well as thofe of the lady.

CHAP. XXIX.

VARIOUS were the opinions of both fexes on this part of his Lordfhip's conduct. We fhall therefore make no comments upon it, but leave every reader to form his own judgment upon fo very extraordinary an event.

The purpofe for which his Lordfhip kept a feparate houfe being now ended, he, immediately after this adventure, took his beloved home again to his own houfe, where fhe was vefted with every authority as miftrefs of it, and as fuch was obeyed, treated, and refpected, for upwards of three years, at the end of
which

which time, his Lordfhip was appointed governor of a neighbouring
kingdom.

This noble appointment filled our
heroine with the higheft tranfports.
She knew fhe fhould thereby have
an opportunity of vifiting her native
foil, and providing for feveral of
her poor friends and relations. The
neceffary preparations being made,
his Lordfhip fet out for his government, and took *her Excellency* with
him, but as he could not, with
any propriety, take her to the ufual
place of refidence of the *Vice Roys*
of that kingdom, a certain courtier,
(who was then heartily tired and
afhamed of the name he was born
with, and therefore warmly follicited
for

for a title, which he has since obtained, having a delightful *villa*,
within a few miles of the capital,
made his court to our heroine, not
doubting but it was the proper channel for preferment, and requested
she would honour his feat with her
refidence, during *her Vice-Royfhip*,
which *was gracioufly accepted.*—The
name of this place is Luttrelftown,
where she kept a very brilliant court,
and received as many addreffes and
memorials, as the firft goveinor of
that, or any other kingdom. She
indeed filled her part of the adminiftration with the greateft dignity
and applaufe, and became as remarkable, and as univerfally refpected for
her generofity and compaffion, as
for her patriotifm and profound fkill

in

in politics. She was, in short, the *Maintenon* of the age.

Amongst many other instances of her generosity, we shall mention one that is a recorded fact. There was at that time in the university of the metropolis, a young student, whose name was Wright. His father was a clergyman, who enjoyed a considerable living in the church for many years; but having a large family, to whom he gave a genteel education, he died, leaving little or no fortune amongst his children. And this young gentleman having studied very hard for a fellowship, it was, on examination, given against him, as he thought, through the partiality of the Provost; and having by that

N   means

means loft, or given up, all hope of
preferment that way, he became defperate, and refolved on the following extraordinary method of pro-
motion.

He repaired one morning to our
heroine's court in the country, and
requefted an audience, which was
granted him. He explained the injuftice done him by the Provoft of
the univerfity, and his other circumftances as above related; and declared, as he had no method of procuring an honeft livelihood, that if
her Excellency did not procure him
a commiffion in the army, within two
days, he would then commence high-
wayman, and rob man, woman, and
child, until he fhould be appre-
hended,

hended, as he would, he faid, much rather be hanged than ftarved. Our heroine, ftruck with his refolution and addrefs, prefented him with a purfe of guineas, took down his name and addrefs, and promifed he fhould hear from her fhortly. She accordingly went to his Excellency, and reprefented the affair to him exactly as it had happened, and gave him the young gentleman's addrefs; requefting at the fame time that fomething might be done for him, as he feemed a young fellow of great fpirit and refolution. His Excellency immediately fent for the Provoft, and enquired into his character and conduct, and finding both altogether irreproachable, he inftantly fent an enfign's commiffion to Mifs Faulk-

ner,

ner, who prefented it to this heroe, with a purfe of 100 guineas to buy him regimentals and other neceffaries; and he has fince, through his patronefs's favour, been raifed to the rank of a captain of dragoons, which he·now enjoys.

CHAP. XXX.

ON enquiry into her own family aﬀairs, ﬁe found both her parents were dead, and had left a ﬁon unprovided for, who lived with a gentleman near the place of his nativity: this brother ﬁe ﬁent for, and ordering him to be cloathed and properly dreﬀed, he made his appearance at court, but a few degrees above *Peter the wild boy.* He was, however, immediately put under the care of a tutor, to inﬁruct him as well in letters as behaviour, and in a ﬁort time he could make a very decent bow, and return a civil anﬁwer to any queﬁion that was aﬁked him. Miﬁs Faulkner could hardly be

N 3 per-

perfuaded he was her brother; for there was fomething in his nature, as well as in his fhape, fize and manner, fo clumfey and uncouth, and fo very oppofite to her own delicate frame and temper, that fhe dreaded it was an impofition on her to make her receive him as her brother, until fhe had proper teftimonials of his birth, &c.

After much pains and inftruction, he was, however, introduced to the prefence of his Excellency, and was *gracioufly received*, but how to provide for him was the greateft difficulty Many confultations were held for this purpofe; when it was at length determined to advance him in the army, and a commiffion was

accord-

accordingly given him. He was dreffed in very elegant regimentals; and, by his conftant attendance at his fifter's *court*, and the conftant inftructions he received, with the additions of dancing and fencing, he became very much improved in his manners and converfation, and was permitted to dine at the fame table with *her Excellency*, *when alone*.

We muft not fuppofe that, in this high ftation, our heroine was unmindful of her uncle and aunt *Paragraph*; fhe really was not. She had not been long fettled in *her government*, when fhe fent for them; and they were no lefs furprized than rejoiced at feeing their dear, long loft niece in fuch an exalted fphere of life. Their

N 4   darling

darling hope of title and preferment
was once more revived, and Mr.
Paragraph assured his Lady, that he
always entertained the greatest hopes,
nay was quite certain, that the dignity
of the *Paragraph* family would be
raised by his accomplished niece.
Certain it is, that Mr. *Paragraph*
was introduced to his Excellency at
Luttrelstown, and that he was promised the honour of Knighthood
before the departure of his Excellency from the administration of that
kingdom. But his evil genius still
attended him in the pursuit of this
title, and at the moment he was most
sure of having it conferred on him,
an unlucky and unforeseen adventure, once more, snatched the laurel
from his bended brow. And as it
cannot

cannot be doubted, but every com-
paffionate reader entertains the higheft
concern for the frequent difappoint-
ments of Mr. and Mrs. *Paragraph*,
the circumftances attending this laft
misfortune muft be agreeable to them,
and are for that reafon *only* related in
the following chapter.

N 5

C H A P. XXXI.

IT happened that Mr. and Mrs. *Paragraph*, about a year before their niece's arrival in Ireland, had some occasion to go to London, and, in their passage to Parkgate, were in the most imminent danger of being lost, and the ship wrecked. Mr. *Paragraph*'s greatest concern was about his worthy Lady, and in the midst of the terror and confusion, which the danger occasioned amongst the passengers and sailors, Mr. *Paragraph* was quite composed, and resigned to his destiny. He used every means in his power to cherish and comfort Mrs *Paragraph*, who was almost expiring with fear, and the cries and

shouts

shouts of the numerous paffengers on
board rendered the fcene truly horrible. But this did not in the leaft
affect Mr. *Paragraph*, he was a
perfect philofopher; and retiring
with his Lady to a private corner of
the cabbin, took the moft affectionate
adieu, and at the fame time affured
her, there was one thing which he
could wifh to be refolved in before he
left this world, and that her anfwer-
ing him a fingle queftion would fet
his mind perfectly at reft, and fit it
for a paffage to the Elyfian fhades.
Mrs. *Paragraph* with aftonifhment
affured him, there was nothing that
fhe could do to contribute to his
repofe or happinefs, which fhe would
not chearfully comply with, and

N 6   defired

defired him to explain himfelf; which he did by the following queftion:

"I beg then to know whether my dear Mrs. *Paragraph* has ever been falfe to my bed?"

Which queftion produced the following reply:

"My contempt, Mr. *Paragraph,* for the prefent fhail conquer my indignation. If you were not confcious of fome defects on your part, you would not have dared at any time, but particularly on fuch an occafion as this, to have afked me fo prefumptuous a queftion; nor will I anfwer it otherwife than by affuring you, that whatever has happened,

3   relative

relative to your mean fufpicions, fhall remain a profound fecret in my own bofom, *fink* or *fwim*."

In all probability this converfation would never have been repeated, had not a certain paffenger been lying in a hammock juft near them, and in the dark they could not perceive him. Mr. *Paragraph*, confounded and abafhed, left his lady to get on deck, and learn whether he fhould be allowed further time to dive into this impenetrable fecret, which he had fo much at heart; and to his great joy was informed, they were all out of danger, and ready to land, which they did a few hours afterwards at Parkgate; and he hoped and be-lieved, that his cabbin converfation was entirely forgot by Mrs. *Para-graph*, and that he fhould never hear more about it nor did he ever after, until he was upon the very point of his knighthood.

Hear, gentle reader† and fympathize in the misfortunes of this worthy man. The perfon that heard the cabbin converfation, was no other than the inimitable, fatirical, and wicked Mr. *F——*; and Mr. *Paragraph* having about this time a difpute with the manager of one of the theatres in Dublin, the cruel and malicious *F——* was tempted, *by fome infernal inftigation*, to introduce this converfation, with fome other fevere ftrictures on the perfon and character of Mr. *Paragraph*, into his Orators,

which

4

which rendered him so perfectly ridiculous, that for some months he never went out of his own doors, without being followed by a parcel of boys and rude mob, mimicking this cruel mimick, in the character of Mr. *Paragraph*, and asking him, *whether his dear Mrs.* Paragraph *had ever been false to his bed?*

Although it is perfectly disagreeable to relate, yet it is true, that there never was a character exhibited, *Cadwallader* not excepted, that afforded so much diversion, or met with so much applause. Mr. *Paragraph* could not be persuaded, that F——— could be so inhuman, as to render him an object of such ridicule, and for his conviction, was persuaded by
some

some arch-rogue to get into a private part of the house, and have both ocular and auricular demonstration; which he agreed to. But no sooner had he taken his seat than he was surrounded by such crowds, that he could not get out, of which the cruel F—— had intelligence, and added some strokes of wit and satire, which let the audience know that Mr. *Paragraph* was present, which drew such bursts of applause and laughter, as almost deprived that worthy gentleman of his senses. He got home, and instantly complained to his niece, but neither her authority, nor that of the *Vice Roy*, could suppress the performance for upwards of twenty successive nights.

Mr.

Mr. *Paragraph* at length had recourse to the law, and preferred a bill of indictment againſt Mr. F——— for libelling him, which the grand jury immediately found, and by that means the piece was for the preſent ſuppreſſed; but the affair had ſuch an effect on Mr. *Paragraph*, that he would not have attended before his Excellency to be dubb'd for the firſt title in the kingdom, and has ever ſince remained *plain* Mr. *Paragraph*.

C H A P. XXXII.

THIS unlucky incident gave our heroine much anxiety, but she conducted herself with great moderation and prudence, and, in the course of *her administration*, acquitted herself to the entire satisfaction of the whole kingdom. But, after her return to England, she had a pension settled on that establishment, of six or seven hundred pounds a year on one Mr. L———, whom the people of that country never saw nor heard of, and have never since been able to find out, *and for that reason* many in that kingdom, as well as in England, have been malicious enough to report, that this pension is established

blifhed for *her own ufe*; and that fhe
receives it to this day; which has
greatly altered their fentiments both
of her and his Excellency.

Granting this were true, is it not
very furprizing, that thefe ungrateful
and unnatural people fhould murmur
fo much at paying a few hundred
.pounds a year to a gentlewoman of
their own country, who rendered
them many fignal fervices during *her
adminiftration amongft them*, when
they at the fame time, without reluctance, pay upwards of a hundred
thoufand pounds a year, in places
and penfions, to the *Sardinian Ambaf-
fador*, *Dicky Riggabout*, *Blackard
Hamilton*, and many other honourable and right honourable rafcals,
whom

whom they have never feen nor heard of, unlefs when they come among them, to enflave and plunder them ?

It has been often remarked, that it is impoffible for *ladies*, who have any hand in the adminiftration of national affairs, to preferve their integrity, that is, that they are more liable to what is vulgarly called bribery and corruption, in the felling and procuring of places, employ-ments, &c. &c. than men; or at leaft that they do it, *with a much better grace*; and it is reported that our heroine, after her return from her *Vice Royfhip*, became fo fkilled in this art and myftery of politicks, that fhe planned out the channel for her Lord's being appointed to one of the

moft

moſt honourable and lucrative employments in this kingdom, in the
conduct of which it is whiſpered,
that ſhe has acquired an immenſe
foitune for her and many of her
attendants.

Her brother, whom we muſt now
diſtinguiſh by the name of Captain
F———, returned with her to England, and ſhortly after obtained a
company of foot; and as ſhe was
determined to make him the head of
her family, ſhe employed ſeveral
agents to find out ſome rich citizen's
widow or daughter, with whom ſhe
could ſtrike up a match. She at
length found out a widow lady, who
lived near Bloomſbury Square, and
who had an only daughter, extreamly
beautiful

beautiful, and intitled to a fortune of 20,000l. This lady, whose name was C———r, was the widow of a stock-broker in the city, who had acquired an immense fortune, and had left his widow as rich as his daughter. In this family our heroine determined to provide for her brother, either with the mother or daughter, and for that purpose got into the acquaintance of some of Mrs. C———r's friends, who knowing her influence over Lord H———, and how much it was in her power to promote both them and their friends, thought themselves highly honoured in her acquaintance and visits, and Mrs. C———r and her daughter were soon admitted into this party. Even

in

in *this company*, great apologies were neceffary to be made for the roughnefs and crudity of the Captain's behaviour, but it was obferved, that he had always been at fea, or in the field, ever fince his youth, and it could not be expected, that the joint production of *Mars* and *Neptune* fhould be modernly polite, tho' acceptable even to a *Venus*. Mifs C——r was really an elegant girl, and was now in her twentieth year, but had never had any opportunity of keeping polite company, and had received but an indifferent education; yet fhe could not but entertain an utter averfion to this heterogeneous monfter. His bulk was enormous, his complexion and countenance horrible, and his behaviour and converfation

resembled

resembled that of a wolf, more than a
human being, no wonder then that
this lovely girl could not endure him.
But on his part it was entirely otherwise; he was enamoured with her
from the first moment he saw her,
and pressed his sister, in the most
earnest manner *he was able*, to forward
his pretensions.

C H A P. XXXIII.

IT is true, Mrs. C———r gave this amiable Captain all the encouragement he could wifh for. But in order to vindicate her character, it is neceffary to obferve, that Mifs C———r had fome time befoie taken a fancy to hei mothei's coachman, and eloped with him for a whole week before fhe was difcovered and taken back from him, and tho' Mifs C————r affured her mother and all her friends, that the coachman was *too modeft* to make any attempt on her virtue, yet her mother was under apprehenfions, that fomething more had paffed that might be productive of very *vifible*

O   confequences

confequences in due time, or that her
conftitution was too warm for the
climate of London. Thefe confiderations, together with the honour and
advantages of the intended alliance,
induced her to give the captain all
the encouragement he could defire;
and as the finifhing ftroke to this treaty, Lord H———— in perfon waited
on Mrs. C————r, and affured her
of his countenance and protection on
the occafion. This was an honour
not to be refifted, and Mifs C————r
was ordered to hold herfelf in
readinefs for the captain's embraces.

They dreaded the averfion Mifs
C————r expreffed to her lover,
and although Mifs Faulkner never
paffed a day that fhe did not vifit
Mrs.

Mrs. C———r and her daughter, or had them down with her at Lord H———'s country feat, fhe could not procure Mifs C———r's confent to the nuptials. On the contrary fhe declared, fhe would fuffer death rather than marry the man fhe de-tefted. But as the captain was fure of the mother's confent and 20,000l. he gave himfelf very little concern about the inclinations of the young lady, provided he got her into bed to him, which his fifter and Mrs. C———r promifed him he fhould have. Under thefe circumftances it was thought moft advifable to have a fpecial licence, left fhe fhould prove refractory at church, and mar their defigns; but with the fpecial licence fhe could be noofed at Lord H———'s country feat

by

by his chaplain, by force or any other means they could devise or should find necessary. A special licence was accordingly obtained, and every thing prepared for the ceremony

Miss C———r suspected their designs, and had for some time past entertained an affection for a young gentleman, that lodged directly oppo-site to her mother's house, but had never had an opportunity of speaking to him but once, tho' they had often conversed with their eyes from the opposite windows. To this gentle-man she was determined, at all events, to apply for assistance, and as she was never permitted to stir out of doors but in the company of her mother and other attendants, she was

under

under the neceffity of writing to
him; and after acquainting him with
her melancholy fituation, fhe frankly
owned fhe had for fome time loved
him, and was ready to put him
in poffeffion of her perfon and fortune.

This young gentleman had for
fome time looked on Mifs C———r
with a favourable eye, but being
informed that fhe was juft on the
point of being married, he thought
it idle to give himfelf any farther
trouble about her, and for that reafon
had neglected to pay that attention to
her frequent appearance at her window to him, and fome other fignals,
which this information only prevented
his confidering in their true light;

O 3 but,

but, on receipt of her letter, he was determined to refcue her out of the houfe, at the peril of his life. He accordingly bribed her maid to deliver his anfwer to her letter, defiring that fhe would be ready to elope that night at eleven o'clock, that a chaife and four, with proper attendants, fhould wait within a few yards of her door, and that he would be ready to receive her the moment fhe fet her foot out of the houfe; and drive off directly for Scotland.

The receipt of this letter rejoiced Mifs C———r to fuch a degree, that fhe could hardly contain herfelf; nor did ever poor maid fo much long for the appointed hour. She could not reft

a

a moment in any one place, but run into every private room and corner of the houfe, to read over and kifs this warrant for her delivery. Night came, and her lover ftood at his own window, looking at this lovely girl putting on a light riding drefs, and juft preparing to fteal down ftairs, when lo! her virago mother entered the room, and feizing her in the moft brutal and violent manner by the hair, dragged her about moft inhumanly, and threatned to murder her. No man of either courage or humanity could ftand to fee fuch barbarity. Her lover flew down ftairs, and thundered at Mrs. C————r's door, but was refufed admittance. The treacherous maid,

O 4　　　　who,

who carried the letter, was in pay with Mifs Faulkner, and difcovered the whole defign to Mrs. C———r, who had previoufly fent off an exprefs to the captain, barricaded and locked all her doors, and would not permit any perfon to enter, until the arrival of the captain and his fifter. But fhe no fooner faw the young gentleman knocking at her door, than with a true Billingfgate vociferation, fhe cried out, Thieves ! Murder ! Rape ! Ravifhment ! Robbers ! Watch ! Help ! Neighbours ! &c. &c. for a full half hour, without once ftopping, till her breath was quite exhaufted, and fhe became fo hoarfe, that fhe could not baul out any longer. Her cries alarmed the whole neigh-

neighbourhood, and the houfe was prefently furrounded with numbers of people. This in courfe obliged our young heroe to decamp, to his inexpreffible grief and mortification.

C H A P. XXXIV.

THE unfortunate Mifs C———l's
hopes of delivery being thus
fruftrated, her lover, whom we fhall
call Mr. Butler, fired with love and
refentment, was refolved to fupport
his pretenfions by his fword; and as
foon as he faw the Captain enter
Mrs. C———r's houfe the next morning, he fent him a card, defiring he
would appoint a time and place,
where he fhould wait on him that
evening. The noble Captain fhewed
this card to Mrs C———r, who inftantly conftrued it into a challenge;
and told the Captain, that this was
the very fellow, whom her daughter
was going to elope with the preced-

ing

ing night, and advised him, by all means, to decline meeting the *ravish-ing, blood-thirsty rogue.* These were really her expressions, and it is but just the reader should have them by way of instruction, and as a specimen of polite education. This explanation of Mr. Butler's card threw the Captain into the utmost consternation. It is true, he had for some time wore a sword, but had never yet been called upon to use it; and, on due examination of himself, he discovered an utter aversion to cold iron. He was therefore very easily persuaded to follow Mrs. C——r's advice in declining to meet Mr. Butler, or even to send him any answer to his card, until the arrival of Miſs Faulkner—*who was now of the privy council.*

During theſe deliberations, Miſs C——r was locked up in a dark cloſet, and a guard ſet over her; and about noon Miſs Faulkner drove up to Mrs. C——r's door in Lord H————'s coach and ſix, with a ſplendid retinue of ſervants and attendants; and being informed of the buſineſs of the night, and reading Mr. Butler's card, ſhe inſtantly declared, ſhe would have that raviſhing villain taken up by a ſecretary of ſtate's warrant, and impriſoned for life, for daring to conſpire, or threaten the death of her brother, who was then ſo immediately connected with the ſtate; and accordingly

ingly set out for Whitehall for that
purpose: but upon stating the affair
to Lord H———, his Lordship
was of opinion, that he could not
with safety issue a warrant against
Butler, as Captain F——— had not
yet been sworn into the privy council. He therefore recommended a
warrant from the civil magistrate, for
apprehending Mr. Butler.

Before this warrant could be obtained, it was necessary, that the
Captain should appear before a justice
of the peace, and swear, *that he was
in dread and fear of his life*, from
the terrible menaces of this assassin,
Butler; which, to the honour of his
regimentals, long sword, and valiant
cockade, he certainly and absolutely
did

did do, and obtained a warrant
againſt Mr. Butler, who was taken
thereon, and bound over in a re-
cognizance of 5000 l that he would
not commit any aſſault on the mag-
nanimous captain; and when the re-
cognizance on the part of Mr. Butler was entered into, the magiſtrate,
as uſual in ſuch caſes, recommended
it to Mr. Butler, to bind the Captain in a like ſecurity to keep the
peace with him. Mr. Butler told
the juſtice, that he could not do
it; and being aſked his reaſon, he
ſaid, that as it could not be done
without his ſwearing, that he was in
dread and fear of the Captain, it was
impoſſible he ſhould do ſo without
perjuring himſelf, for that he was
not in dread or fear of any thing
like

like him; and giving the Captain a
look of the highest contempt, left
him at the justice's.

This point of honour being thus
settled, it was resolved that no more
time should be lost in the accom-
plishment of their design. Miss
Faulkner therefore. prevailed with
Mrs. C——r to take her daughter
with her immediately into the country, and that the nuptials should be
celebrated the very next night. The
wretched Miss C——r was accordingly released from her confinement,
and by force put into Lord H——'s
coach, with the valiant Captain;
and they set out directly, with a
magnificent retinue, for B——y Park,
where the next night the heroe was
put.

put in poffeffion of one of the fineft girls in England with a fortune of 20,000 l.

It would fhock humanity to read or defcribe the barbarities, that were practiced on this unfortunate young lady, to force her into the arms of this monfter. Let it therefore fuffice to fay, that in lefs than a month they feparated. Her averfion to him every hour increafed, and fhe juftly treated him with abhorrence and contempt; which fo provoked his brutal nature, that he beat, kicked, and abufed her almoft every hour: and as they returned to Mrs C——r's in fome few days after their marriage, the whole neighbourhood was alarmed in the middle of the night

with

with this diftreffed lady's cries of Murder. Several gentlemen forced into the houfe, and on entering her room, found her weltering in her blood, beat and bruifed in the moft fhocking manner, and her fine hair, torn out by handfuls, ftrewed about the chamber. Her monfter of a hufband was treated with the utmoft indignity and abufe by feveral of the fpectators, particularly by one gentleman, who directly took his wife out of the houfe to his own, and the next day generoufly had her fituation laid before the Lord Chancellor, who ordered her an immediate maintenance, fuitable to her fortune, and ftopt the noble Captain's receiving a fingle fhilling belonging to her — until a further hearing.

Mrs.

Mrs. C——r, when it was too late, saw the cruelty of her behaviour to her daughter. She immediarly agreed to the feparation, and went into the country with her, but the treatment fhe had received, made fuch an impreffion on her tender heart, and fo affected her, that fhe fell into a deep confumption, and at the end of fix months died; leaving her mother and the detefted Captain to difpute her fortune; which, perhaps, they are, at this day, contending for in Chancery. It is poffible, the gentle reader will wifh, that neither of them may live to enjoy it.

C H A P. XXXV.

THE death of Mifs C——r, and the difappointment of re- ceiving the 20,000 l. which our he- roine expected the Captain fhould pocket with her, were fevere ftrokes both to her pride and political views. Lord H— ——, notwithftanding his high and lucrative employments, was in the moft embarraffed circum- ftances; nor was it an uncommon thing to fee an execution, with a parcel of ruffian bailiffs, lodged in his houfe, and his plate and furni- ture on the very point of a public fale. The greateft part of the 20,000 l. was therefore intended to be lent h' Lordfhip *at intereft*. The

dif-

difappointment fell heavy; for many
of his Lordfhip's creditors, who
were to have been filenced out of
this *finking* fund, became clamorous:
and the pay of a captain was by
no means equal to the appearance
and expenfive plan of life, which
the brother was neceffarily obliged
to fupport during his courtfhip; and
now that he was involved in a fuit
in Chancery, he was once more become an abfolute dependant on the
generofity and courtefy of his fifter
and Lord H————. The latter
never much liked him, though he
faw and received him, in compliment to his adored Mifs Faulkner;
but this lady, being ftill refolved
to force his fortunes in the world,
frankly fhared the *Irifh* penfion with
him

him for fome time, and fupported
his caufe in Chancery, which rendered his circumftances tolerably
eafy.

Hitherto Mifs Faulkner had acted
with much caution and difcretion
in the courfe of Lord H———'s
adminiftration; that is, fhe was not
very exorbitant in the prices or conditions, on which fhe granted and
procured feveral valuable and lucrative employments; but whether from
neceffity or avarice, we cannot determine (though inclined to think
fhe was influenced by the former) fhe
now played both an open and a
defperate game. Her former generofity and prudence at once forfook
her. There was no office, no employment

ployment, in any one department, to be diſpoſed of, but through her means and procurement; and on theſe ſhe fixed her own price. Enormous ſums were raiſed through this channel of negotiation, and where money was not to be had, bonds, annuities, and dividends of the profits and income of each employ were daily executed and ſecured, till at length her office became a public exchange, and her brokers were as well known as thoſe at *Jonathan's* or *Lloyd's*.

During this noble adminiſtration, Mr. D————n heard of the power and riches of his lady, and though in poſſeſſion of a very genteel income abroad, he was reſolved to ſhare ſome

of

of the fpoils at home; and accordingly arrived in England, at a time
when his prefence was neither expected nor defired. After he had
fpent a few days in London, con-
fulting with his friends, and inquiring
into the real fituation of his wife's
finances and prerogative, he made
her a formal vifit at Lord H———'s
houfe in Great G———ftreet. It
is but reafonable to fuppofe, that his
fudden appearance before his lady
and Lord H———, muft have
ftrangely alarmed and difconcerted
them His Lordfhip expreffed both
the greateft furprize and refentment,
and demanded his reafon for quit-
ing his employ, without his knowledge and permiffion: to which
Mr.

Mr. D————n replied, that the falary of his office was fcarcely fufficient to fupport him, and that he could not reconcile it to himfelf to be banifhed from his native country, and all the other pleafures of life, for a bare maintenance; that he was well affured, Mifs Faulkner had it in her power to beftow fomething confiderable upon him, without hurting herfelf; and that his Lordfhip had it alfo in his power to promote him to a more agreeable and profitable ftation than that which he then enjoyed; and he concluded with fome difagreeable infinuations, in cafe his terms were not immediately complied with.   3

Mi.

Mr D————n was not only peremptory but exoibitant in his demands. Several ſtratagems were made uſe of to evade his pretenſions, but he had ſagacity enough to eſcape every trap that was laid for him; and as Lord H———— now dreaded a ſeparation from Miſs Faulkner more than any other earthly curſe, Mr. D————n's de- mands were, at length, complied with. He received a conſiderable ſum of money in hand, and a much moie advantageous and honouiable employ, than he was formerly poſ- feſſed of, and immediately retuined to the Weſt Indies, where he has evei ſince iemained, without inteı- rupting the happineſs of his lady and Lord H————.

P   If

If we were at liberty to urge, that the favourable or unfavourable events, that happen to us in this life, are proportioned to our virtues or vices, it might be concluded, that thefe fafhionable lovers were adequately mortified and punifhed for the mutual indulgence of a criminal connection, by the fudden alteration both of their circumftances and reputation. Lord H——had been always efteemed a man of great abilities, integrity, and honour; and had formerly filled feveral confiderable departments of the ftate, with the higheft applaufe. But he had now near finifhed his political career. The rapacioufnefs of his miftrefs, and his indulgence, or connivance at the bare-faced depredations

predations fhe daily committed, drew
upon him the juft and fevere cen-
fures of the publick; in fo much
that he became both defpifed and
detefted · and his former reputation was now inveloped in the
deep fhade of his follies and vices.
His neceffities obliged him to act,
in one of the moft confequential
employments under the crown, not
agreeable to his own good fenfe
and extenfive abilities, but as the
tool and flave of a perfon, the
moft obnoxious to the whole kingdom. He had no will, no power,
but what he received from an
odious Favourite, who has fince
abandoned him to the public refentment, and the perfecution of

almoft

almoſt the whole nation; the conſequence of which is likely to reduce him to beggary*, as well as infamy. His diſtreſſes have forced him to take from his miſtreſs all her ill-gotten treaſures, and he now lives with her in the country, in obſcurity, where they indulge their mutual paſſion, and their ſole ambition is to provide ſome fortune for a daughter, the only pledge

---

* The reader will perceive, that the above paragraph was written before the deciſion of the cauſe between Mr. Wilkes and the Earl of Halifax, where the damages awarded by the Jury, fell ſo much ſhort of public expectation, and where it appeared, that theſe damages, though ſo unconſcionably ſmall, are to be paid, not out of his Lordſhip's pocket, but out of the national treaſure

of their shameful connection. His Lordship is, however, under the strongest engagements to make Miss Faulkner Countess of H————, as soon as the death of Mr. D————n can render such an union practicable.

SUP.

SUPPLEMENT.

*The following Anecdotes came to hand
after that part of the Memoirs, with
which they are immediately connected,
was printed off, and where, if they
had been admitted at all into the body
of the history, they ought properly to
have been inserted. They are therefore here given by way of Supplement, nearly in the same words in
which they were communicated to the
publisher.*

Mr. BINGLEY,

AS you are about publishing the
Memoirs of a celebrated Lady,
if you have any empty space left,
you are heartily welcome to the
following Anecdotes, upon the truth
of which you may safely depend.

" When

" When Lord H———'s Seraglio was tranſported to Ireland, amongſt the other appendages of his houſhold, his favourite Sultana was accompanied by ſeveral ladies of eaſy virtue, who, being married, added no ſmall ſanction (as they thought) to the moſt profligate ſecret meaſures, and the moſt daring treſpaſſes upon all public decency and decorum.

" Henry K——ne (a contented cuckold) now of Golden Square, architect, and firſt gentleman of the bed-chamber to his Lordſhip, retained no ſmall influence in the cabinet through the intereſt of his wife with the Sultana, as did alſo another of the bed-chamber, whoſe name I have now forgot, through the intereſt of his wife with the ſame Sultana, for which

he'

he was rewarded with a finecure petty government of 400 l. per annum in fome interior part of Ireland, which he now holds by deputation; and his Lordfhip not having then an immediate opportunity of providing for Mr. K—ne, did, without the leaft fcruple or fhame, create a place for him, unheard of before, at the expence of the public, by making him Surveyor to Dublin Caftle, &c. with the capacity of receiving in England, the falary annexed of 500 l. per annum, without any obligation binding him to crofs the herring-pond, to fuper-intend the duties of this nominal office *. Thefe acts of

---

* This occafioned a late fpirited enquiry in the Houfe of Commons in Ireland, which made his commiffion fhake, but did not overthrow it.

muni-

munificence in his Lordſhip weie followed by two others more gracious, though leſs meritorious, viz. He gave an employment (at the inſtance of the above-mentioned lady) to Mr. Uchſide Offley, Mrs. K—ne's favourite, and her huſband's journeyman, in a double capacity; and transformed hei brother (by the power of his Lordſhip's magic wand) from a ſtone-maſon, into a ſon of Mars, by complimenting him with a lieutenant's-commiſſion in the army; from which, (if not mortgaged) he now receives half-pay.

" When his Lordſhip acted in one of the firſt offices of the ſtate, Mrs. D——l—n appointed the celebrated Mi. S——rd, her ſecret broker, the infamy of whoſe character is too.

well

well known to ftand in need of any illuftration. This fellow had the audacity to blufter about from coffee-houfe to coffee-houfe, in the face of open day, negociating and tranfacting every piece of dirty bufinefs, that could bring the Sul-tana ten pounds, and twenty fhil-lings to himfelf; and had the ad-drefs to obtain, through her means, an enfigncy in the Royal Scotch, when commanded by Sir Henry Erfkine, for a *petit maitre* fon of his; and alfo a confulfhip for Cap-tain Buckmafter, his fon-in-law, which he now holds in one of the Barbary States.

I am, Sir,

Your humble fervant,

CIVIS."

To Mr. BINGLEY.

Dublin, January 2, 1770.

SIR,

I FIND by an Advertisement in the News-Papers, that you intend publishing the Memoirs of Miss Faulkner, now Mrs. D————; and as I suppose you mean to give some account of her present keeper, Lord H—l—f—x, the following Anecdotes, I presume, will not be thought unworthy of a place in the History of that Lady.

Soon after his Lordship was preferred to the government of Ireland, Mrs. D———— (who was then in England).

England) was apply'd to by Mrs L——m (a very remarkable Lady here) in favour of her hufband. No fooner did his Lordfhip receive Mrs. D———'s letter on this fub-ject, than ftraight way Mr. L——m was dubbed Governor of Rofs Caftle Had he been an object of charity, his Lordfhip's bounty would have been well beftowed, but fo far was this from being the cafe, that thefe peo-ple affume all the pride and parade of people of fafhion, and yet could meanly condefcend to beg from a creature, who, but a few years ago, was an inferior ftrolling actrefs in every fenfe of the word, and even now, in all her glory, has nothing more to boaft of, than being the kept miftrefs of a man, who has

made

made himfelf odious to the whole
nation, by violating the rights of
the Britifh fubject. But what is all
this to his Lordfhip, his miftrefs,
or their dependents? The government of Rofs Caftle has riveted Mr.
L——m his friend, and the wife
and miftrefs are fworn fifters. They
vifit and re-vifit, and Mrs. L——m
don't look upon Mrs. D———n's
being an adultrefs *now*, as any crime,
becaufe fhe's fure, if D—— were
dead, his Lordfhip would make her
an honeft woman, though that, I
confefs, I very much doubt; for
(believe me Sir) D—— might be
prevailed upon to fue for a divorce,
if they came up to his price, nor
would there be any thing more extraordinary in his cuckolding his
Lordfhip

Lordſhip after marriage than before, as it is generally ſuppoſed he hath often done ; for I have been informed, that his viſits to his wife, when ſhe lived in Mancheſter Buildings, were very frequent.

Lord H———— was next apply'd to by Mrs. D—— for ſomething (as ſhe term'd it) to a woman of a very extraordinary character, a Mrs. Penelopy V——tr, a creature held in the loweſt eſtimation upon the ſtage, which was her profeſſion. She took the name of Miſs *Danvers*, from her murdering Indiana in the Conſcious Lovers. She has bulk enough to bear more being ſaid, but her connexions and abilities are too inſignificant to merit any further notice.

In

In fhort his Lordfhip granted her
a penfion of (I think) one hundred
pounds per annum, which, with the
penfion that Mrs. D———— has under
a fictitious name, gave great and
juft caufe to the people here to
murmur. They even talked of
abolifhing all fuch penfions; which
I hope they will one day or other
have power and fpirit enough to do.
A government and two penfions, beftowed upon fuch worthlefs wretches,
were deemed meafures the more excep-
tionable, as there were many real ob-
jects of charity at that time in the
kingdom. There were then, to my
knowledge, clergymens and officers
widows, who had no other fubfift-
ance, than what they could raife by
benefit concerts every year. How
amiable muft his Lordfhip have appeared,

peared, had he appropriated the
above emoluments to their ufe!
Shame it is that two idle ftrollers,
of the loweft clafs, fhould rob our
diftreffed natives of what ought to
be allotted for their fupport. As
his Lordfhip dwells much upon his
private feelings, thefe, as well. as
other acts of injuftice, clearly fhew
his total want of focial virtue: elfe,
the joy he muft have felt at doing
a really benevolent action, would
have made him fo happy for the
day, that it would, in my mind,
have doubled his pleafures for the
night.

The next noble act he performed
within my knowledge is as follows.
There was a Quarter-mafter in the
fifth,

fifth, or royal dragoons of Ireland, whofe name was Paulfrey. This poor man went fecurity for a gentleman, for (I think) 300 pounds. The man dying foon after, the Quarter mafter- was arrefted and confined for the money, which it was not in his power to pay by any other means than the fale of his warrant, which was all he had on earth (at that time) to fupport himfelf, a wife and eight children. The poor fellow, well knowing his inability, contrived to make his efcape. He flew to his regiment, which received and protected him. The Sheriff of the county made application to the Duke of Bedford (our then Lord Lieutenant) to order the officers to give the Quarter-mafter up ; but upon the

the worthy man, who was Lieutenant Colonel of the regiment at that
time, hearing of the request made to
His Grace, he immediately went and
begged for mercy, which the Duke
very humanely granted. The poor
man remained quiet for some time,
but when the mighty H——— came,
he ordered him to be given up to
the rage of his creditor. Happy had
it been for some in England had
his Lordship met the same fate.
The Colonel, with his usual good-
nature, interfered again, and told the
whole affair truly as it was, and
earneftly begged for a certain time
for the payment of the money; but
no favour could be obtained. His
Lordship had been apply'd to by a
member

member of parliament, and the affair *muſt* be done.

The Colonel then ordered the man
to town, and entertained him in his
own houſe for at leaſt ſix months,
during which time his Lordſhip promiſed he would make ſome proviſion
for him, provided his commands
were complied with; nay even
pledged his *word* and *honour* for it.
The Colonel, who had no idea of
any man forfeiting either, was happy.
The warrant was ſold (to great
diſadvantage) the debt paid, and
the poor man little better than a
beggar. Perhaps you are juſt going
to bleſs his Lordſhip, thinking
there's another government for him.
But ſtop a little. He was poor,
and

and could not follow the golden rule, nor was his wife honoured with the acquaintance of Mrs. D——, consequently he was not an object worthy his Lordship's notice. Soon after Lord H—— got on the other side of the water, but left his *word* and *honour* behind, for I don't find he ever carried either the one or the other back with him. It was recommended to the Quartermaster to sell them, but they were so blotted and stained, that not a single soul here would be seen to purchase them. In fine, they hung so heavy upon the man's hands, that he mustered up all the cash he could borrow from his friends, and set out for London to have the *honour* of laying them,

with

with all duty and obedience, at
the Earl's feet. But though he
was there for two years (and in
such diftreffed circumftances, that
he muft have perifhed, had it not
been for his old friend the Colonel,
who happened to be in England,
and again affifted him, as he always
thinks it incumbent upon him to help
the diftreffed) and had been both
at his Lordfhip's town and country
houfe, yet could he never get a
fight of him except in the ftreet.
In fhort, the Colonel was obliged
to fupply him with twenty guineas
to bing him back to his family;
and he brought his Loidfhip's *word*
and *honour* back with him, and
as he could not make a penny of
them, they were hung up at the
entiance

entrance of the caſtle, to ſhew
every nobleman (I had like to have
ſaid gentleman) that entertained the
ſame principles, that they need not
pawn their own *word* and *honour*, as
they might have Lord H———'s
dog cheap.

But, Sir, I muſt farther ſhew
you how fond his Lordſhip was of
preferring people of merit.   There
is one B———m, who originally was
a cobler in a little town they call
Laughray. He afterwards enliſted
as a trooper, and being a ſneak-
ing artful fellow, got from one
thing to another, till he became a
ſort of a riding maſter ; and when
Lord H· ——— came, he found
                            the

the method of creeping into his
and his nephew's good graces; for
when ever Sir G—— rode, B——
would fwear he was one of the
beft horfemen he had feen; nay,
made him believe he was a demi-
god, and rode upon the clouds:
but when he turned his back, would
damn him, and fay it was impoffible for any mafter to make him a
horfeman. However this B——m
has a fon, a mighty infignificant
fellow, and of a very indifferent
character. As for example, he very
frequently affifts his father in beat-
ing and abufing his mother; nay,
has often turned her out of doors.
This I had from her own mouth,
and I give it you for fact.   I
only

only mention this circumstance to
shew his and his father's merit.

Nevertheless, to the amazement
of every body, he got a Cornetcy
in the regiment already mentioned,
which is held in the highest esteem
here. The story went *then* that
his Lordship made him a present of
it; but the story goes very different *now*. Five or six hundred
pounds have been given upon such
occasions before now, and though
these people must have been pushed
to the last extremity, to raise such
a sum, yet if it was required, one
would stretch a point upon such an
occasion; and if a man has a nephew, and cash scarce, 'tis a very
pretty sum (let me tell you) to

warm

warm one's fingers with on a winter's morning. This fame Cornet, or (perhaps by this time) Lieutenant B——— is fo exceedingly clumfy and awkard, that he is a difgrace to the regiment, as moft of the officers are very handfome fellows, and all not only gentlemen's *fons*, but really gentlemen themfelves. How far fuch a fon, of fuch a father, had pretenfions to a commiffion in this regiment, I'll leave you to judge. I am told his merit confifts chiefly in the theatrical way, as he is an excellent mimick, by which means he recommends himfelf to the corps. Though he has had no education, he fets up for a fine gentleman; but (as Mr. Haladay,

Q the

the clergyman, faid to him) he had better ftudy to make both Ends meet, as his father had done before him; alluding to the cobbling bufinefs.

I am, Sir,

Your moft obedient fervant,

An IRISHMAN.

F I N I S.

Ingram Content Group UK Ltd.
Milton Keynes UK
UKHW022042140323
418589UK00004B/59